CW00368843

Don't Die Wondering

Stunning photographic portrait of
Happy Clapper by Sarah Ebbett.
(Courtesy Sarah Ebbett Photography)

The
Pat Webster Story

Don't Die Wondering

"From a drover's son to a Group 1 winning
trainer ... and a champion called
Happy Clapper"

As told to Alan J. Whiticker

NEW
HOLLAND

First published in 2019 by New Holland Publishers
Sydney • Auckland

Level 1, 178 Fox Valley Road, Wahroonga 2076, Australia
5/39 Woodside Ave, Northcote, Auckland 0627, New Zealand
newhollandpublishers.com

Copyright © 2019 New Holland Publishers
Copyright © 2019 in text: Alan J. Whiticker
Copyright © 2019 in images: AAP, Alan Whiticker, Sarah Ebbett and The Webster Family
Front cover images © AAP
Back cover images © Alan Whiticker

All rights reserved. No part of this publication may be reproduced, stored in a retrieval
system or transmitted, in any form or by any means, electronic, mechanical, photocopying,
recording or otherwise, without the prior written permission of the publishers and copyright
holders.

A record of this book is held at the National Library of Australia.

ISBN 9781760791872

Group Managing Director: Fiona Schultz
Publisher: Fiona Schultz
Project Editor: Elise James
Designer: Yolanda La Gorcé
Production Director: Arlene Gippert

Printer: Toppan Leefung Printing Limited

10 9 8 7 6 5 4 3 2 1

Keep up with New Holland Publishers:

 NewHollandPublishers

 @newhollandpublishers

Contents

Gerry Harvey

I started in the horse racing business back in 1972, and I have been giving people horses to train ever since. I spread my horses with about fifty trainers across Australia and New Zealand, when most people in my position have just one main trainer.

I'll never do that. I'm an equal opportunity owner.

Theo Green was one of the first trainers I approached to train for me, and he recommended a hungry young Randwick trainer named Pat Webster. That would have been at the end of the 1970s.

My wife Katie Page says I'm attracted to people who have an interesting story because I listen to them and give them a go when other people don't. Pat is a good example of that.

Pat Webster has always been one of my favourite trainers, if not my favourite. He's a good bloke and 100 per cent trustworthy. I would never expect him to tell me something about a horse that wasn't exactly what he thought. He has always been upfront like that.

That's why I've given him horses for forty years now. We've had a lot of good horses in that time, but no champions. That's okay; it's not the end of the day.

But I always have high expectations because I think Pat is as good a trainer as anyone in the game. And the good thing is, he now has Happy Clapper to prove it.

Pat is a self-made man. When you get to know him, you realise he didn't have the advantages others may have had in life, and yet he's made the most of his talents. He's also a great role model for others and a wonderful ambassador for racing.

We need people like Pat in racing because he has the ability to influence others, especially in his mentoring of young jockeys. The most satisfying thing in life is developing people around you and seeing them do well, and Pat is no different in the work he does on and off the track.

Everyone in racing is genuinely happy for Pat's Group 1 success with Happy Clapper. He's been working with horses all his life and the universal opinion is: good on him. Well done, mate.

The Pat Webster story is a great Australian success story.

Pat's Story

Pat Webster was not a happy man.

Michael Thomas, the breeder-owner of the best horse in Pat's stable, had just informed the veteran Randwick horse trainer that he was transferring the immensely talented but injury prone gelding Thankgodyou'rehere to another stable.

Not that Michael Thomas was unhappy with Webster's meticulous, hands-on approach with the horse. Thankgodyou'rehere had won eight races and over half a million dollars in prizemoney under Pat's guidance. No, the main reason for shifting the horse to Melbourne was that his new trainer Peter Morgan operated a state-of-the-art water-walker. This one piece of equipment could potentially solve the gelding's ongoing leg problems.

Pat had been in the game long enough to know that losing horses to rival trainers, including the good ones, was part of the deal. But this was different.

'It was 2011 and I was in a training partnership with my son Wayne at the time. Thankgodyou'rehere was special to us ... it was like losing one of the family.'

But there was a sweetener. 'Michael phoned to tell me I was losing the horse, and in the next breath he says, "but I'm going to give you a two-year old I bred". When I asked him what the breeding was, he said the horse was by Teofilo, which I had never heard of, from his mare Busking.'

The rising two-year-old was promptly sent up to Webster's farm at Kulnura on the NSW Central Coast. The horse walked off the float and Pat was far from impressed. 'I put it in the top paddock and I said to my wife, Chrissy, "Well, we've lost a good horse and got a donkey!"'

Days later, Pat had to go to the races so he placed the Teofilo gelding in a lower paddock. 'When I came home from the races Chrissy said, "You know that donkey you were talking about? We'll it's a fast donkey". He was running around the paddock and he could go!'

The Teofilo-Busking colt was named Happy Clapper. Not only would the horse change Pat's life, giving him that elusive Group 1 success all racing trainers desire, but it would also allow him to parlay a lifetime of hard work and industry goodwill into reaching out and helping others. A mentor to young jockeys through his work with Racing NSW, and an ambassador to country racing through the Racing Mates initiative, Pat has a determination to give something back to a sport that has provided him with so much.

'Happy Clapper's success has helped me enormously', Pat says. 'I've been able to do a lot of good with my work with drugs and alcohol counselling because the Clapper put me on the map and gave me a platform to talk to people in need.'

Helping others in the racing community has kept him humble. 'I can go and spend half a day with an ice addict and that will bring me pretty much down to earth, don't you worry about that.'

Pat Webster has come a long way in his almost seven decades on the planet. From a poor beginning in country New South Wales to apprentice jockey and Group 1-winning trainer, the laconic Webster is widely respected by the racing industry. Not only for what he has achieved in his roles on the racetrack, but also because of the work he does behind the scenes.

The great irony of his racing career is that Pat waited all his professional life to get his champion horse, only to have Happy Clapper's achievements potentially overshadowed by the deeds of the great mare, Winx. But that underestimates the determination of the trainer, who took on the might of

Winx eleven times in Group 1 races and watched his horse finish second to her time and time again.

'There are champions and there are freaks,' he would tell the racing media, 'but Winx is a freak'.

In guiding his giant gelding to success, Pat has shown his skill as an astute horseman with the patience of Job. Happy Clapper has amassed almost $7 million in prizemoney for owner-breeder Michael Thomas, and is the only horse to have won the 'Big Three' mile races at Randwick – the Villiers Stakes, The Epsom Handicap and the time-honoured Doncaster Mile.

'The Clapper' has captured the imagination of the racing public and forged his own place in racing folklore. So has Pat Webster.

With a bush upbringing where you 'had to be twice as tough as the elements', Pat found success the hard way. The following newspaper profile from the early 1980s when he was a struggling young trainer reads like a movie script:

> **He could ride before he could walk; he drove 4000 sheep before he was ten. At age twelve, his mother passed away and he entered full stable life in the desire to become an apprentice jockey. He rode his first winner at age fourteen – using a dodgy birth certificate – and became one of the most promising young jockeys in the Western Districts. In Sydney, he was apprenticed to Bernie Byrnes at Randwick and won at Randwick on his first ride there ... (but) before the age of twenty, his career came crashing down when he badly broke his leg in a race fall at Rosehill.**

Pat made a brief comeback, even returning to the bush origins to ride, but the constant wasting was too much of a sacrifice. Married at age twenty-one, with a young wife and son to support, he worked as a track rider, an

PAT'S STORY

advertising rep for a national newspaper, a wharf labourer and a porter for Ansett before starting out as a horse trainer in 1978.

Horses were in his blood. 'The old-timers use to say you would have to have horse shit on the brain to be in this game,' Pat says, 'but once you've got it, you've got it'.

The Webster stable had its measure of success at Randwick, but with a small stable he had to work harder than some to make ends meet. Pat was not a punter, but he knew how to get a horse ready for a plunge and attracted owners who liked to have a bet on the right horse. The stable punched above its weight and the rewards came quickly – the 'Clive Comet' sting in the early 1980s even allowed him and his young family to buy a larger house in fashionable Kensington.

Wife Chrissy made a home for him and their three children, something country hardman 'Spider' Webster and wife Blanche had struggled to do for Pat and his older sisters in country Inverell. Pat and Chrissy's kids went to good schools in the Eastern Suburbs and had an education he could only have imagined. All the while, the Websters looked for business opportunities to better their life – a pork ribs shop, a liquor store, a farm up in Mudgee.

Their motto is 'don't die wondering'. Take a chance. Have a go.

When trainer Theo Green retired in 1988, Webster inherited the majority of his stable including the Group performer At Sea. That horse's success proved to the racing fraternity, and to Pat, that he had the talent to train a good horse. He thought that Ab Initio and Thankgodyou'rehere would finally give him that elusive Group 1 success, but both horses were dogged by bad luck in big races.

And then Happy Clapper came into his life and everything changed, except the long hours, the hard work and the sleepless nights worrying about his horses. That had always been part of Pat's life.

As 'The Clapper' started his winning run on the way to capturing the 2015 Group 2 Villiers Stakes, only to be swamped by the Winx juggernaut, Pat's laidback approach and bush humour resonated with the racing media and the Australian public. There was something of the 'Aussie battler' about the veteran trainer that people liked.

'Life just doesn't throw up good stuff, you have to take the bad too', Pat admitted in a recent interview. 'But not many people know what we've been through. They see the headlines – and it looks like it's all beer and celebrations – but there's actually something much deeper going on that many people don't know about.'

Until now, that is.

A huge part of Pat and Chrissy's life that hasn't been publicly known was the twenty-year battle they waged, along with other members of their family, with their eldest son's drug addiction. Patrick Jnr stumbled into drugs as a teenager and has only just come out of that long hell. It had a profound effect on all of their lives and informed many of the hard decisions they had to make along the way. The most important of these was to raise Patrick's son, Jack, as their own.

Perhaps that was why Peter V'landys, the chief executive of Racing NSW, asked Pat to take on the role of mentor to young jockeys who are struggling with the ups and downs of the racing game … too much money, the influence of 'new' friends and the prevalence of drugs – especially alcohol and methamphetamines. Part of Pat's role is to travel the state and talk to jockeys about success and failure in the most fickle and unforgiving of sports.

Pat was keen to help from the outset and is now an accredited Racing NSW drug and alcohol counsellor. Similarly when Racing Mates, a peer support initiative established by Racing NSW in 2016, appointed several ambassadors across NSW, Pat was one of the first to be recruited. Ambassadors are available when industry participants in the bush – trainers, jockeys, stable hands – need someone to talk to.

'There is nothing better than talking to someone who understands where you're coming from', Pat says.

Through the Webster family's generosity and honesty, they shared these stories with me over many visits to their family property at Kulnura on the New South Wales Central Coast. What shone through is Pat's devotion to his family, his love of the horses in his care – the slow ones *and* the champions – and his commitment to the wider racing community.

'My main motivation in life is to challenge myself. Everything I have achieved has come from nothing – I saw the hardship my parents went through and the question I constantly asked myself over the years was: could I make myself into something?'

Pat Webster has made a life for himself and his family, and much, much more.

Don't Die Wondering is his story.

Alan Whiticker, August 2019

CHAPTER 1

Inverell

Situated in northern New South Wales, on the Macintyre River close to the Queensland border, Inverell could be viewed as one of those typical Australian country towns popularised by artist Darcy Doyle … a picture on your wall of barefoot kids playing cricket on a dirt road outside a weatherboard corner store with a 'Bushell's' sign emblazoned in large letters on the side. But the harsh reality of the post-war country town was somewhat different.

Inverell has always been farming, sheep and cattle territory. But in the 1950s, the river that winds its way through the town divided it into two distinct halves, perhaps best described as the 'haves' and the 'have nots'. Wealthy graziers, the town's business folk and the well-to-do lived on one side of the river, while the other side was reserved for the town's transient workforce, assorted carnival workers and stockmen … and the local indigenous community. They were the 'dirt poor', literally.

Patrick John Webster was born there on 19 February 1951. 'We lived on the corner of Medora Street. The other road was a dirt track which led to the local racecourse, funny enough. On race mornings, my mother would stand on the corner of our block hosing down the road so the dust wouldn't come into our house from the cars driving to the races.'

To say Pat's father, Leslie Arthur Webster, was something of a local legend in Inverell is an understatement. Even today, walk into any pub in the district, as Pat and his family have done over the years, and the name 'Spider' Webster still means something … not just because he was a tough bastard, Pat says, but because of all the people he helped in the community. Spider was a drover, part-time horse trainer and, later, a stock and station agent, buying and selling cattle. He also ran his own transport business for a time, but always had a horse or two in training, forever chasing a dollar at a time when a dollar was bloody hard to get.

As Pat tells the story, his father didn't go off to World War II because he had a misgrown toe that overlapped another on one of his feet. 'He wanted to go, even though he was married and my older sister Fay had been born, because the country was coming out of the Great Depression and a job was hard to find at the best of times. But he couldn't march, let alone run for his life, and so he stayed in Inverell.'

Spider Webster met Pat's mother, Blanche Alena May Burns, at a dance in Pitt Street, Redfern sometime in the mid-1930s. His mother's people originally came from Casino, but Pat doesn't know too much about that side of the family tree. His sister Lesley was the family historian and, sadly, she passed away not that long ago. Fay, some ten years older than Pat, has also passed.

'Thank God mum and dad decided to try for a boy,' Pat laughs, 'or there would be no bloody story to tell'. He was simply called 'The Baby' by his mother and sisters.

At the height of the Depression, Spider Webster was down in Sydney on the lookout for a good horse to take back to Inverell when he met his future wife. Blanche was smitten, and Spider was able to entice her back to Inverell with little more than a promise of a future together. They were battlers, survivors.

'When we lived in Inverell, Mum and Dad would go ballroom dancing at the local hall, wearing a large number pinned on their backs just like the professionals. My older sisters would take me there to watch them through the hall window ... and they were pretty bloody good dancers too!'

Before he left Sydney, Spider was drinking with Kevin Spain, who had the contract to transport horses from the stables to the track for the morning workouts and again on race day. 'Kevin Spain was a lovely man; a real gentleman who was still transporting horses around tracks when I became an apprentice jockey in Sydney in the 1960s', Pat says. 'Dad told him how bad things were in the bush and Kevin said he would lease him a horse named Balmoral and gave £20 as a start. He even offered Dad a lift to the station so he could catch the train back to Inverell.'

Blanche Burns went with him.

The Webster family lived very simply. 'We had dirt floors in our house. People today might think we lived in the dirt, but the clay floor hardened like concrete and polished up like marble. After a pretty bad hail storm, we had sugar bags hanging in the windows instead of glass, and we owned an old fridge with a gaslight underneath.'

Pat promised his mother that he would buy her a modern electric fridge when he made it as a jockey. 'Mum didn't live long enough for me to buy her that fridge,' Pat trails off, before adding with a smile, 'but I did end up training for Gerry Harvey, the greatest fridge salesman in the world'.

People never worried too much about money back then because they had so little of it. The only time one of the kids found a spare penny or thrippence was if they pulled it out of one of Blanche's plum puddings at Christmas. She would save all year to make it, and made sure everyone got a piece.

Pat loves telling young jockeys the story about only owning one pair of shoes when he was a boy. 'And they were my school shoes', he adds. The three Webster children had to go out barefoot each morning and milk the family cow, Saucepan, and her calf Buttercup before they went to school. 'In winter there would be so much frost on the ground as soon as you saw the cow drop a "patty", you would put your feet in the shit to keep them warm.'

But the Websters were optimists at heart, even in the bleakest of times. 'One of the good things that happened when the river flooded was Dad would shoot a duck and bring it home for dinner.'

Life was hard in the bush, and often unforgiving. Riding the bus home from school, Pat would sit on a small box beside the bus driver. 'My mate Terry Creer got off at the stop before me. [One day] when he went inside his home his father was lying on the floor with a gunshot wound to his head. He'd committed suicide.'

By the time Pat got off the bus, Terry was running up the road towards him, calling out, 'Patty, Patty. Come home with me. Something's wrong'.

'We opened the door and his father was lying there, covered in blood', Pat recalls. 'It was a lot to take in for a couple of nine-year-olds, let me tell you. I remember Terry's father was wearing high-heeled riding boots. You don't see many people wearing those types of boots these days.' Pat is still in contact with Terry Creer, who remains another old mate from his hometown.

'Terry's mother married a local publican, so he and his sister were very well looked after and had a good life.' Only recently Pat learned that Terry's father had borrowed Spider's gun to take his own life. 'I suppose it was just all too much for the poor bloke. There were no support agencies in those days.'

Suicide was an unspoken epidemic in many parts of the bush. In many ways, it still is.

But Pat has mainly fond memories of his childhood. 'When the circus came to town one year, the rumour went around that a black panther had escaped and was "knocking off" sheep in the district. We'd be driving along a country road and Dad would tell me to look up in the trees and see if I could see that black panther. It wasn't until years later that I learned that the "black panther" was more of the two-legged variety.'

Sheep and cattle duffing were rife in a time when people struggled for survival. 'When Dad said that he was heading out to "the long paddock", he would invariably come home with a slaughtered lamb or sheep to share with everyone.'

Spider Webster was barely one step in front of the law. 'The police would come to our house looking for Dad. Mum would stand at the door and say,

"I haven't seen him myself for weeks, officer. When you find him, tell him he's months behind in his child support". Dad, of course, would be sitting in the kitchen sipping a cup of tea.'

Closing time at local pubs was 6 pm sharp, and each night Blanche would tell the children that it 'wouldn't be long now before your father gets home for dinner' (10 o'clock closing came in in 1957). Men drank 'middies' of beer and women drank 'sevens' of shandies – a mixture of lemonade and beer. A hardy few drank schooners, often to excess.

Pat's father could drink with the best of them and back it up if needed. Some nights, Spider would come home from the pub with the knuckles on both his hands red raw. 'Mum would sit beside his bed and bathe his hands with saltwater, and then tell me to do the same.'

But living up to his reputation in town would prove Spider's downfall.

'When I was really young,' Pat says, 'Dad fought a bloke out the back of the local hotel and the bloke hit his head on the ground and later died. Dad did a couple of years in gaol for manslaughter for that'. Pat is short on the details, because he was so young when it happened, and it's part of the family history best not dwelt upon. Spider Webster never did.

Being the baby of the family, and the only boy, Pat was doted on by his mother. By his own admission, he was a mother's boy and could do no wrong. His older sisters, though, kept him in line. 'Fay used to take me to the shops and if I tried "chucking a sook", she would sick her cattle dog Boomi onto me. I'd quickly fall into line … that damn dog did everything she told it to.'

When he was about ten years old, Pat contracted hepatitis and was seriously ill for several months. 'The girl who lived next door to us had hepatitis and I remember Mum saying not to go inside their house. The girl was getting better, though, and her mum suggested I come in and play draughts with her to keep her company.' Pat ended up contracting the disease and was desperately ill.

Pat was in a hospital isolation ward for almost three months and lost a hell of a lot of weight. 'The doctors and nursing staff wore masks when they treated me, and Mum and my sisters could only visit me looking through a screen door. I was a terrible shade of yellow, and I couldn't eat any dairy food after that – I still can't eat butter. I came out of quarantine a skinny kid and that's when I decided to become a jockey.'

One day, Pat's father came home and informed everyone that he'd bought the boy a pony. 'My best mate Jack Dixon had a piebald pony which he called Chips, and my pony was a grey I called Tarpot. Jack and me did everything together as boys ... we were like brothers. We rode our ponies all day, bareback of course because we didn't have any money for saddles, often stopping off at the river banks to play soldiers or look for an ant's nest to destroy.'

'Pat was a villain', Jack Dixon recalls. Now retired after working more than fifty years in the local abattoir, Jack stills lived in Inverell, having married and raised a family there. 'He was a rogue, as was I. You had to be to survive in the bush. Our fathers were drovers together, and Pat's mother Blanchey was like a second mum to me. I would often stay and have dinner with the Websters and head off home when it was dark. It was just a different era.'

The boys made their own entertainment and created their own mischief. 'We could have been killed a hundred times over', Jack says.

One on such adventure, Pat almost drowned in the Macintyre River. 'I was about eight or nine,' Pat remembers ruefully, 'and I jumped in, which I shouldn't have'. The current was moving quickly and a local Aboriginal boy named Lance Bartholomew from Tinga dived in and pulled him over onto a riverbank. Pat admits that they didn't have a lot to do with the black community back then, before adding, 'but I'd love to see him again and shake his hand. If it wasn't for him, I wouldn't be here'.

On the Websters' side of the McIntyre River, Inverell was mostly a flat flood plain. Drovers who came to town would often camp there in open paddocks and let their horses graze there while they hit the pubs in town.

First thing the next morning, Jack and Pat would muster all the saddle horses for the drovers, hoping they would get a small tip.

The sales yards were at one end of the racecourse, and Pat and Jack would head up there and ride the calves for a bit of fun on a Friday night when the sales were on. 'We'd nearly get ourselves killed because they had steel yards in those days – with unpadded steel gates. I don't know why we did it, just to be naughty I suppose.'

When the Inverell Show came around every year, Pat and Jack would ride the poddy calves out of the cattle chute to the cheers of the crowd. During the Grand Parade of Champions in the main showring, they formed the great idea of greasing a pig and letting it loose among the livestock and horses. 'It created havoc.' Pat remembers it clearly as being an orange pig with large black patches. The boys hid under the grandstand and nobody ever did find out who let the pig loose. 'There would have been hell to pay', he says.

Pat had learned to box at the local Police Boys Club. At the Show, Jack and Pat would make a track to Jimmy Sharman's Boxing Tent. The fighters would be out the front of the tent, banging the drum and calling out, 'come inside and go a pound a round'. Pat and Jack would hop inside the ring – being the sons of 'local legends' known for riding their ponies around town gave then enough notoriety for Sharman to give them a go.

'We were only boys,' Pat says, 'but we'd have a really good go, flogging each other or some other kid, black or white, and then clean up all the sixpences and shillings the punters through into the ring and then go and spend it at the show. It was good money, too!' Tellingly, on one occasion, Pat asked his mate Jack to let him win a fight because Spider was watching in the wings. The friends shared the money 50/50 anyway.

Living every boy's dream, Pat and Jack started to ride their ponies to school each day. 'I would let Tarpot lose in a vacant paddock next to the corner store opposite the school. I would throw a towel on the pony's back so I wouldn't get my school shorts stained with horse sweat. My mate Jack went to the local Catholic School in town because he was more of a Catholic than I was. The horse would pick all day in the paddock and then I'd ride him home from school.'

Horses, and horse racing, were an important part of the local community. Some local trainers had large stables and there was always a race meeting on the weekend, if not at Inverell, at local towns such as Warialda, Bingara or Moree. 'Mum loved getting dressed up and going to the Inverell races with her friend, Sheila Lawrence, the wife of local jockey Pat Lawrence. A great little rider named "Skeeter" Kelly used to stay with us over the Christmas carnival. He was later killed in a race fall at Glen Innis.'

Trainer George Sinclair would come to Inverell every Christmas with a team of a dozen or so horses and stay at the local showgrounds. 'Dad would say that we were going down to see your Uncle George, and the smell of liniment being rubbed on the horses' legs would almost knock you over. Trainers today don't use liniment to treat horses but that smell takes me straight back to those days.'

One year, one of Sinclair's fillies was set for a maiden race at Inverell; the team had put a lot of work into the horse and it duly saluted. 'I have a funny suspicion this was the same meeting the swab hut caught fire', says Pat. Someone lit the straw placed on the ground to soak up the spillage when the horses provided their post-race urine samples. No swabs were taken that day.

'Perhaps it was just a coincidence', he laughs.

With Spider Webster, it was either feast or famine as far as horse training was concerned. He won a Moree Cup and a Warialda Cup and lots of minor races, but the most he ever had in training was six horses. 'He was not a professional trainer, like today,' Pat says, 'but he was always looking to get a horse fit so he could get a win and earn a quid or two'.

When Spider had a big win, the family would go to Jo Mah's Chinese Restaurant in town. 'As a boy, it was like going to Star Casino and seeing Kerry Packer there', Pat says. 'Everyone who was anyone in town would be there on a Saturday night.' Country life is different from the 'big smoke', he says. 'Everyone knew everyone.'

It was about this time Pat was introduced to show jumping after joining the local pony club, which was run by the McGregor family. There he learned horsemanship, patience and humility. Early on, the group of young riders were told to put their ponies in a large paddock for the night and to water them in readiness for a parade through town the next day. Pat put Tarpot in an adjoining paddock that already had water in it, but during the night his grey pony rolled around in the mud and was more brown than grey when Pat turned up the next morning to ride him through the main street.

'There was not time to wash him,' Pat rues, 'so Mr McGregor made me ride a dirty horse through town. It was quite embarrassing really because everyone knew me'. It was an early life lesson for the future jockey and trainer. No cutting corners.

But the McGregors saw something they liked in the young rider. They recruited Pat as their star junior rider and taught him the ins and outs of show jumping. They also had access to the best show horses in the district, especially 'flag racing' horses. 'All you had to do was sit on them and the horse did all the work', Pat says modestly. 'Going from a pony to a horse was amazing. They were big strong bastards with a great turn of foot.'

The McGregors kept the prizemoney ('Not that much,' remembers Pat, 'just enough to feed the horses and make ends meet'). Pat collected the ribbons, and lots of them. 'I won a lot of ribbons, which my wife says I should be proud of', Pat says. His mother made them into a rug for him, which he still has, and he is certainly proud of that.

But the horses, Pat maintains, were the real stars.

CHAPTER 2

A Drover's Son

In the 1960s, the stock routes used for droving sheep and cattle to market were still an open range, especially in northern New South Wales and southeastern Queensland. This was years before routes were cut off by farm fencing and the urban sprawl from the larger townships. Trucks were still a scarcity, so drovers were employed to drive stock to sales yards in the tried and tested Australian way immortalised in such films as *The Sundowners* and *The Shiralee,* and the poetry of Henry Lawson ('The Ballad of the Drovers') and Banjo Patterson ('In the Droving Days').

Spider Webster was many things to many people, but he prided himself on his skill as a drover. Work was hard to come by, however, and he would disappear for weeks on end trying to earn a quid. He had dabbled with truck transport since the mid-1950s, and learned to handle a truck on the long treks to market, packed with sheep or cattle, but the old ways were still the best.

In the winter of 1963, Spider took a huge gamble and invested all he had in droving 4000 sheep from Inverell to Goondiwindi, a large town on the northern side of the NSW-Queensland border that would later be immortalised as the home of the great grey galloper, Gunsynd. It was the sort of gamble where a small fortune could be made, and the fate of an entire family could turn on the toss of a coin.

Young Pat was in his first year of high school when his father told him he could either stay in school and be cared for by his sisters, or come droving with him and his mother. His oldest sister Fay was already married and

Lesley had left school to start work in a local store. 'I didn't have to think twice about it. I hated school and longed to be outdoors. The only thing I liked about school was playing rugby league for the school team. I couldn't leave quick enough.'

It would also come at an important time in Pat's young life, and in the married life of his parents, although he didn't know that then. Pat's mum was in the early stages of an illness that would claim her life within twelve months.

'Mum and Dad slept in a caravan while I camped in the back of the truck with several indigenous lads who came along with us on the drive.' The best part of the drive, as he remembers it, was his mother cooking in a camp oven every night. 'The other guys were pretty good bush cooks too, but they weren't a patch on mum.'

The drive would take a couple of months and Pat was expected to complete school by correspondence, picking up packages of lessons mailed to local post offices along the way. 'The indigenous blokes were a lot smarter than me and they ended up doing most of my school work.'

The Aboriginal stock hands also taught Pat how to better control a horse by riding on a 'long' rein. 'Horses were just so relaxed for them, they just responded really well to the balance of their bodies', Pat says. 'We want to rein horses in tight, but they were just casual, athletic riders.' They could roll a cigarette with one hand, get a box of matches out of their top pocket, light the cigarette and still have control of the horse with the other hand, Pat observed, although he never mastered that particular trick.

'They were young blokes in their twenties or early thirties', Pat remembers. 'Lovely guys, happy go lucky.' But old biases still operated in the bush. When the drive approached a country town, Spider would camp outside the district for the night. Only then would he go into town to buy a few longnecks of beer, and bring them back to share with the others because he was afraid that if the stockmen went to town and hit the pubs, they wouldn't come back.

'Dad really believed that,' says Pat, 'but he had the drive to think about. It was a huge gamble for him'.

During the drive, the family's caravan tipped over and locals from town helped the Websters get back on their feet. 'I remember a Father O'Brien helped us, so Spider said to him, "Seeing you helped me, Father, would you Christen my lad?" The priest threw some water on me, then and there, and it was all done. I didn't get a say in it'.

This was no Hollywood movie or sentimental bush poem. This was real life, and the harsh reality of the Australian bush was never far away. Halfway through the drive, the ewes birthed their lambs. If they were left lagging behind on the long drive to the sales, they could just as easily fall victim to crows pecking their eyes out and wild dogs at night. The solution was just as brutal, especially for a twelve-year-old.

'The lambs were killed when they were only days old', Pat says matter-of-factly. 'The indigenous stockmen would hit them on the head with a nulla-nulla and that was that. We would leave them stacked in piles under a tree because we just had to keep going.'

Worse was to follow. Just before they came into Goondiwindi, located on the northern side of the McIntyre River which snakes its way north and forms part of the NSW-Queensland border, the sheep came down with a disease colloquially called 'yellow big head'. Rams butting heads in a large herd are suspectable to a virus (cholangiopathy), which spreads quickly through the ewes, inflaming their head and neck area, and making them look jaundiced and act erratically.

Pat still remembers that day clearly. 'As we were going across this bridge with the river flowing under it, the sheep were jumping to their deaths because the disease had made them crazy. We were just on the outskirts of Goondiwindi when he lost much of the stock. We had been on the road for so long and to see the sheep jumping into the river really broke my dad. These deaths knocked the numbers about and he finished up losing money on the drive.'

'Spider was a hard man, but I saw him cry that day', Pat says, shaking his head.

After the drive to Goondiwindi, Pat's father had to chase work to clear his debts. Pat remembers it as 'a terrible time'. They had lost the family home in Inverell, he had to say goodbye to his mate Jack and even his beloved pony Tarpot. 'I ended up giving Tarpot to a girl in town because I knew she would look after him', Pat recalls.

It was also the time Pat's beloved mother fell gravely ill.

While the family was still living in Inverell, Blanche developed breast cancer. With limited hospital facilities in the bush, especially to treat cancer, Pat's mother had to make the long journey to Sydney for treatment. Pat often went with her. 'We would catch the big black and white bus to Glen Innes, take the train to Central Station and catch another bus to Greenacre, where we stayed with mum's sister while she received treatment.'

Treatment for breast cancer at the time was both radical and intrusive, eventually resulting in a double mastectomy. 'I've often felt over the years, why did she have to take that slow ride to a city hospital on the bus and train? It was a lot of travelling to do to get that done to you …'

The only positive memory Pat can muster from that period relates to older sister Lesley. 'When the Beatles came to Australia in June 1964, they didn't mean that much to me because I was only thirteen years old. But Lesley had a big poster of the Beatles on the wall of her bedroom and was determined to see them when they played at Sydney Stadium. She had already left school and was working in Inverell, so she bought a ticket, took that same bus we took to Glen Innis and caught the train to Sydney.'

It was a journey Pat and his sisters made often with their mother in the last year of her life.

Spider, Blanche and Pat moved to Dubbo, 450 km south of Inverell on the Newell Highway, and lived in the local caravan park with Spider's brother and his wife while he drove a stock and station truck. 'I used to go with dad on some of his stock runs,' Pat says, 'helping him by hanging the manual indicator arm out the window when we turned left'.

The move to Dubbo was not only the end of Pat's idyllic family life in Inverell, it was also effectively the end of his childhood. Rather than send his son to a new high school, Spider arranged for Pat to start his jockey apprenticeship with local trainer Trevor Wrigley. Pat's mother was so ill by this stage, she was hospitalised and didn't know that her son had left home to become a jockey.

At age thirteen, Pat was always going to be tall for a jockey, but he was still very thin and his horsemanship was beyond question. But the real question that needs to be asked was: why wasn't this lad in school? A modern sensibility would view Pat's apprenticeship at such a tender age as the same as being handed over into a form of enforced servitude. Pat's working life had begun.

'That's where I was first introduced to racehorses, having graduated from ponies and show jumping', he says, although he wouldn't get a chance to ride in a race until sometime later. 'I rode a lot of trackwork, though. A horse would bolt on you and you'd been going out hard at a thousand miles an hour hoping not to fall off. I'd be hanging on for dear life and Trevor would be yelling out, "Just steer him son, just steer him … don't try and pull him up!"'

Wrigley trained for local businessman Bill Prendergast, who was his only client. His property had a small track where the horses were trained, but it was actually a working egg farm that they operated as a side business. Pat lived in a converted garage on the property – with a cement floor, Pat points out, which was as cold as an icebox in the middle of winter – with the other stable hands and jockeys.

Being the youngest there, Pat was subjected to beatings and mistreatment from the older boys. 'Gee, I'd like to run into some of those guys now and see how they got on in life.' The only plus was finding an ally in the trainer's teenage daughter. 'She ended up helping me with my correspondence lessons', he smiles. 'It was the only way I could have got them completed with all the work we had to do on the farm.'

It was a tough life, raking out the stables and doing trackwork, especially for a lad who was barely a teenager. 'After our morning chores we would be wiping the shit off the eggs with a wet rag and putting them in cartons.' He hadn't signed on for that, and early on in his life he showed a rebellious streak by putting a couple of eggs down the exhaust funnel of Bill Prendergast's pride and joy – his bright red tractor. The tractor, of course, wouldn't start.

'I just wasn't happy there', says Pat. 'And you wouldn't believe what they gave us for breakfast. Fried eggs on toast … every day!'

Pat was provided with a modest wage for the work he did on the farm. Soon he had enough money to buy a decent pair of riding boots in preparation for his first ride. The prevailing wisdom at the time was that you couldn't be a jockey if you had big feet. Pat still only takes a size nine shoe, but he was already self-conscious about his height and deliberately bought smaller shoes to delay the inevitable growth spurt.

'I got a lift into town to buy a new pair of riding boots and bought a smaller size six. I wore them walking home, thinking I'd get a lift from someone, and ended up walking miles and miles in them. My feet were a mass of blisters by the time I got back to the farm.'

One of the other boys at the farm told Pat to pack the shoes with wads of wet newspaper, saying that when it dried, it would stretch the leather. 'And that's what I did. It wasn't as if I had the money to go out and buy another pair of shoes and I couldn't very well take them back having walked home in them.'

Pat wouldn't get the chance to put his new boots to good use in a proper race for some time. His life changed again, irrevocably, one morning when Trevor Wrigley came into the communal breakfast area and told Pat he was going to take him into Dubbo to see his father.

'Dad was doing the washing up when I got there. I can still remember the colour of the dinner plates he was cleaning … blue and white. He sat me down and simply said, "Your mother passed away last night".'

Pat, along with his sister, had gone to see his mother in the hospital a couple of days previously, but she was heavily medicated. 'She kept saying to my sister, "The baby has something in his eye". I was lying at the bottom of her bed with tears running down my cheeks. She was in just so much pain.'

The loss of his mother at such a young age, especially one who had doted on the baby of the family, had a profound effect on Pat, even if he couldn't appreciate it at the time. Jack Dixon, who later caught up with his mate again when Pat was a young jockey in Sydney, says: 'You can't imagine what a huge jolt that would have been to lose your mum when you're that age … especially a wonderful person like Blanchey was. She had a tough life'.

This loss would impact Pat on an emotional level too, forcing him at a young age to be independent, intuitive and a quick learner. The shy kid quickly developed a dry sense of humour underpinned by a 'bush' sensibility – common sense, fairness and decency.

Soon, Pat would be on the move again. Spider had bought a truck and was moving to Trangie, 80 km east on the Mitchell Highway, to live in an annex behind the Jackaroo Hotel. Webster Snr was a hard man trying to put the past behind him, but he was not going to leave his only son in the company of strangers. After nine months with Trevor Wrigley, Pat moved to a small township called Geurie, 30 km to the south of Dubbo, where Spider had asked local trainer Betty Lane and her husband 'Tiger' Holland to take over the boy's apprenticeship.

It would be the start of a relationship that would last more than fifty years and change Pat's life forever.

***

In the early 1980s, when Pat Webster was a struggling Sydney trainer, he took Spider back to Inverell to attend a funeral of an old mate. Father and son had retained ties in the town; Pat had returned home to finish his jockey's apprenticeship after his bad fall in Sydney and, after turning to training, had sent horses there when they couldn't make the grade in the city. Spider had also returned to Inverell over the years, although it was decades since he enjoyed his heyday there as a local horse trainer and drover.

After the service, Pat and Spider stopped for a drink at the Imperial Hotel with trainer Pat Begley and stud owner Col Smith. A young man came over to where the group was drinking and asked Pat's father straight up: 'Are you Spider Webster?'

'I am', Webster Snr replied, without looking up from his beer.

'You killed my father', the young man said coldly.

Pat couldn't believe it. 'Fuck me, the guy was 6'3" if he was an inch, and Dad was already in his 60s. Spider says to him, "Look son, I'm not here for any trouble. I'm here for a funeral", but, as Dad used to say, alcohol turns sparrows into emus and guy was looking for a fight. He kept needling Dad, going on and on about what happened to his father, and getting drunker and drunker.

'Finally, Spider said, "Alright then, let's go out the back".'

The fight didn't last long. 'The bloke made the mistake of walking in front of Dad as they exited the back door of the hotel and started to take his coat off. Spider pulled him by his coat and spun him around and dropped him then and there with one punch.'

Pat got his father out of the pub straight away and jumped in their car, an old FJ Holden. 'I just drove and drove and drove, just to get Dad as far away from there as possible, until I just couldn't drive anymore. I finally pulled over when the road was covered by fog and I couldn't see a thing. Dad was asleep in the passenger side of the car, so I stepped out and got some fresh air'.

It was only then that Pat realised they were parked outside Bathurst Prison.

Spider Webster could never escape the past, but his son could.

CHAPTER 3

A Bush Jockey

Betty Lane is today regarded as the 'Grande Dame' of Australian racing, after becoming the first woman to be granted a trainer's licence by the Australian Jockey Club. But back in the early 1960s, when Lane first made her application to the AJC, they turned her down flat. 'After I put the application in,' Lane later recalled in an interview, 'I'm called to sit in front of this horseshoe table and all these dear old gentlemen looking over their horn-rimmed glasses. "Sorry Miss Lane, it's not our policy to license women"'.

Betty was still desperate to be a racehorse trainer so she decided to go 'bush'. She had been told that there was a woman trainer in the Western Districts of NSW and so decided to relocate to Geurie, just outside Dubbo, where she had friends in the local racing industry. When Betty arrived there, she learned there was indeed a woman horse trainer in the district but she still operated under her husband's name.

Lane would use her own name, and gain the patronage of local owners to build up her stable. Within a couple of years, she was the premier trainer in the Western Districts of New South Wales and dominated racing in the area for the next decade before moving to Sydney in 1976.

Lane's husband, Warner 'Tiger' Holland, was a promising bush jockey when he met his future wife in Dubbo. Holland was also partially deaf, and after being denied a jockey's licence to ride in Sydney, he became Lane's trackwork rider, stable foreman and partner. He also acted as an on-course race-caller when the situation arose. It was not unusual for Tiger to finish a race covered in sweat and quickly put on a coat and go out and call the next race in which he didn't have a ride.

Tiger Holland was a character, a racing knockabout. He became so popular in the district they called him 'The Mayor of Geurie'.

'Tiger taught me how to ride', Pat says. 'I was so privileged. He taught me about balance and pace and everything about riding … all the tricks of the trade as well, and there were certainly plenty of those in the bush in those days.'

At Geurie racetrack, for example, there was a dip in the back straight. Tiger warned Pat that rival jockeys would grab a horse's saddlecloth and get a tow into the race before they swung into the straight. 'Tiger said if a jockey did that, pull the stick and give him a whack over the arm. There were not too many stewards at the tracks in those days, let alone cameras.'

When Pat arrived at Geurie after his apprenticeship papers were transferred to Lane, Tiger took him under his wing. Pat lived in a caravan at the back of the stables, but the days of correspondence school were over. Pat was a fully-fledged apprentice. While Betty Lane was the boss and a strict disciplinarian, Tiger Holland, who was only in his late twenties, was more of a benevolent big brother than father figure.

'Tiger used to call me "Aloysius" for some reason. Betty would call out our names, keen for us to do one chore or another, and Tiger would say to me, "Let's just stay here in the stables a little while until the storm blows over, young Aloysius"'.

Tiger Holland was also a budding trainer, and he too would take out a trainer's licence when Betty Lane relocated to Randwick in late 1970s. While wife Betty was winning training premierships in the bush, Tiger would often turn his hand to getting horses ready for picnic race meetings.

'I loved going to the "picnics"', Pat explains. 'Anyone could bring a horse out of the paddock (the animals had to be grass fed) and get them ready for a picnic race meeting. Tiger would get half a dozen horses ready and have a bit of success there.' Pat would attend the races as a strapper, and he recalls one picnic meeting at Wellington where Tiger was the course broadcaster.

'Betty had a horse in a race and I was the strapper. Tiger was broadcasting from the stewards' tower, which was well before the finish line. A group of horses flashed across the finish line, including Betty's. Tiger calls out, "Photo!" in his broadcast but there were no photo finishes at the picnic races. I ran over to the tower and called up to the box, "Tiger, who won?"

'"We fuckin' did", Tiger replied. We actually got beat a long neck.'

When Tiger felt Pat was ready, he took him to Wellington to ride for his jockey's licence. 'The steward there was a guy called Jim Meehan, who finished up a chief steward in here in Sydney. All I had to do was trot the horse down the straight, turn him around and go evens up the course. Then Jim says, "Okay, son, you've got your licence". Today, apprentice jockeys have to ride in twenty or more barrier trials before they get to ride in a race.'

Pat was a quick learner too … well, sort of. 'Tiger told me to keep my knees tucked in when I first started riding. Because I thought I knew it all, I didn't listen to him. So, Tiger put half my wages under one knee and the rest under the other to see how I went on a horse at trackwork.' The money was blown to the four winds.

'When I saw him at the end of the week at the bowling club, he yelled out, holding up a longneck, "This one's on you, Aloysius. You paid for it!"'

Tiger had another surprise for young Pat. Betty Lane had a team of horses in at Gulgong, near Mudgee, on the day of Pat's 14th birthday – 19 February 1965. 'It was my job to unload the horses. Tiger came out of the stewards' room and said, "Come on Aloysius, you're riding today". I told him I wasn't old enough, not having turned fifteen, but he said Dad had taken care of that and doctored my birth certificate.'

Tiger didn't tell Pat he was going to make his race debut before they left Geurie so as not to make the lad nervous. 'Lucky I always had my gear handy, and Tiger was great in giving me whatever gear I needed. I was pretty light at the time so I had to use a heavy exercise saddle to make the weight.'

Pat's first ride in a race was in a Flying Handicap on a horse called Valley Royal. 'Light blue colours with a dark blue sash. There were only four runners in the race. A senior jockey named Johnny Nestor – his grandson Peter Nestor is now a trainer in Dubbo – leaned across and asked me, "Have you every ridden in a race, son?" I said no sir, I hadn't. He said to be careful then. If you jump too quick you can get caught up in the starting wire. "That's what happened to me", he says, lowering the handkerchief he had wrapped around his neck and showing me a large scar around the front. "I jumped too quick and the wire lifted me right out of the saddle."'

The experienced jockey had tried to intimidate the boy by planting a seed of doubt in Pat's mind before the race. It almost worked.

When Pat got around to the starting position, he saw what the older jockey meant – the starter's 'tape' that stretched across the track where the horses lined up was made out of wire, not ribbon or rope. There were very few barrier stalls at many country racetracks in the 1960s.

'Tiger really wanted to beat Johnny Nestor – he and his wife Judy were Tiger and Betty's main competition in the district. Judy Nestor also trained horses, but on race day she'd dress up to the nines and mix with the local committee people. Betty was more comfortable in RM Williams!'

Betty Lane also had another string in her bow. 'Betty was also the official photographer on track. She would then use cotton buds to hand colour the silks on the jockeys with ink.'

A jockey named Timmy Webster (no relation) was teed up by Tiger to look after Pat in the race. 'I drew the rails, Timmy was on my outside and Johnny Nestor outside him. I was hesitant at the start and leant back on my horse and lost a length because I didn't want to get necked by the starting wire. There was no running rail in the back straight, just bamboo flags to guide us, before we hit the straight. Timmy was calling out to me, "Come on son, kick up … kick up", so I came through underneath him. Then he called out, "Ease up now, ease up", and I relaxed. As soon as we entered the straight, he yelled, "Go now, son. Go for home!" and off I went'.

Pat's first ride in a race was a winner. When they came back to scale, Timmy Webster had finished second, about a length behind. As soon as the other Webster saw the chief steward, he said, 'Sir, I'd like to protest'. It was a light-hearted gesture, perhaps to mask the fact that he had given the young jockey some help in the race, but it didn't go down too well with the local stipe.

'Jockey Webster,' the steward said, 'I know you're only joking but if you keep that up, we'll fine you for lodging a frivolous protest'. The jockey kept schtum.

'That was my first experience riding in a race. I have a picture of the win around the house somewhere. An old girlfriend from the bush recently sent it to me.' Still his harshest critic, Pat looks at the photo and says, 'I am riding too long'.

Spider Webster was never that far away, guiding the boy and looking out for potential rides. 'Dad always had an eye out for me. He would drink with the trainers in the public bar at country race meetings and pick up rides for me.'

Pat attended the Parkes Cup meeting with his father one year, even though he didn't have a ride on the day. 'I always took my gear with me, just in case. Dad came over to me and asked what weight could I ride? There was a horse called Golden Draw that had only 7 stone 7 lbs (47.5kg) in the Cup and they needed a lightweight jockey. I was claiming seven pounds as an apprentice – another three kilos – and I doubted I could get down to that weight and I told him so.'

Spider told Pat not to worry about the weight. The scales used at Parkes were ordinary bathroom scales. Pat was told that when the clerk of the course hangs his red coat on a hook next to the scales, he should tug on the sleeve of his jacket with one hand to lessen the weight when he weighed out.

'What happens if I win?' Pat asked. Spider said for him not to worry. The clerk of the course returns to scale and hangs his jacket in the same spot.

Golden Draw duly won at 33/1, leading all the way easing down. 'It was the only animal that walked into the ring with a winter coat – it was that hairy – but when the gates opened it just took off and won by a length and a half.' Another fan recently gave Pat a copy of the race finish when he attended the Parkes Cup as part of the Racing Mates initiative. 'And I looked pretty good sitting on it too', he says.

A big win often meant a 'sling' from a happy owner – ten or twenty pounds perhaps, which was a lot of money at the time – but for Pat, money never came into it. 'At age fifteen, I never even worried about money. Betty and Tiger paid me a weekly allowance and we had a lot of success together.'

Pat plied his trade in the bush for the next two years, riding his claim down from seven pounds to two. He rode against the best riders in the district; Ned Dougherty, 'Spike' Jones, Merv Sing Ho, Harry Williams, and 'Doc' Logue, the father of Maurice Logue, whom Pat would later work closely with at the Racing NSW Apprentices School.

'I rode against Tiger in many races too. One day we were in the jockeys' room and Tiger asked me to go and see the bar steward and ask for a small bottle of dry ginger ale. "Tell him it's for me", Tiger told me. I found the steward and asked for the dry ginger ale for "Mr Holland" and took it back to him. I later found out it had a nip of scotch in it. The old jockeys used to say that it helped them lose sweat, but it was really to settle their nerves.'

Betty Lane had a runner in at Orange one day, and Tiger pulled Pat aside and told him the favourite had drawn barrier 14. 'The money's on and the jockey is taking no prisoners. He'll cut you in half to get across to the fence so don't be handy at the jump.'

'It was rough and tough, knock 'em down riding, so you learned pretty quickly. The jockey knocked down half the field and won the race while I finished third or fourth. The jockey got a six-week suspension, but only because the starter gave evidence against him for what he saw happen at the start'.

Betty Lane was easily the best trainer in the district, with a degree of horsemanship and skill that put her above the rest. 'The prevailing theory about training horses in the bush seemed to be "train 'em like a drunk; just put the bridle on and let them go".' Pat says. Betty Lane changed all that.

But it was Tiger Holland who moulded Pat into a young rider of considerable promise. He was a mentor for the boy, in good habits and bad.

'I had a wonderful time with Tiger. We'd go into town on a Friday and Tiger would have a few beers and I'd get to drive Betty's new Toyota station wagon home from Dubbo, even when I wasn't old enough. Tiger would say, "You drive home Aloysius and I'll do the gears". Thank God it was only a country road.'

Years later, in 1978, when Pat became a trainer at Randwick, Betty and Tiger had already relocated there after the AJC had finally granted Lane a trainer's licence. In 1990, Tiger was also granted a trainer's licence there. They remained close friends with Pat and Chrissy until Tiger's passing in 2008, aged seventy. Pat Webster delivered his eulogy.

'Tiger never spoke a bad word against anyone', Pat told a packed congregation at St Jude's Anglican Church in Randwick. 'I was apprenticed to Betty Lane at Geurie when Tiger was still riding but essentially, they were a team … I had just lost my mother and they took me in and I stayed there until I came to Sydney three or four years later.

'Everyone loved him. He could even make (fellow trainer) Jack Denham laugh.' And that was some feat.

In 1967, Spider Webster decided to move to Sydney where he had contacts for a job on the docks. 'Dad said now was the time to come to the city.' The boy was quickly out-riding his claim in the bush but, to get ahead in a tough game, he had to ride against the best and that was in Sydney.

Pat Webster had enough of a reputation as a promising bush apprentice for his father to approach Randwick trainer Bernie Byrnes about taking him on. 'Dad set that up,' Pat says, 'although I was fairly well known by then, having ridden a lot of winners. It was actually to both our benefits for

Bernie to have an experienced apprentice in his stable because I could still claim my allowance and obviously, the racing was so competitive.'

Spider Webster left the bush for good, driving an old Holden station wagon all the way to Sydney with a couple of mates in the back seat.

Teenager Pat Webster was beside him.

CHAPTER 4

The Big Smoke

In 1967, Pat Webster was a sixteen-year-old apprentice jockey trying to make his way in a world of men. 'Even as a claiming apprentice it was tough to get rides in Sydney. You were lucky to get one ride a week in town because the competition was so tough.' This was the era of George Moore, the champion jockey of the 1960s, and Des Lake, Kevin Langby, Peter Cook and Jack Thompson.

'Ron Quinton won the apprentices premiership one year with about twenty wins in the city wins,' says Pat, 'and even in my best year I had no more than seven wins in town'. As an apprentice jockey living on a monthly stipend, money was always tight and winners hard to come by.

Pat lived with other jockeys above Bernie Byrnes' stables at historic Newmarket. 'Bernie had an office at one end of the stables with a ladder outside leading up to a flat where he stayed. There was then a series of individual rooms with a shared toilet and bathroom for the jockeys. We rode trackwork, mucked out the horse boxes – and Newmarket had the biggest boxes in town, let me tell you – and waited for our opportunity to ride in a race.'

The 'big smoke' was a change of pace for bush-bred Pat Webster – even catching a taxi or a bus was an adventure. 'I had a great mate called Kerry Pankhurst who was apprenticed to Doug Lonsdale at the time. Without him I might not have survived in the city and would have gone home to the bush. We'd head off into town, go to a dance at Waverley at night or visit a Chinese restaurant. We weren't really into the social scene – we were apprentice jockeys and horses and riding were our world.'

But there was another world waiting when you opened the gate at Randwick, Pat says, and he was keen to explore it. Pankhurst, fellow apprentice John Quinlan and Theo Green stable hand Ken Stone helped him burst the racing bubble he was living in.

Pat rode mostly at the midweek provincials, and most weekends too, in order to get a ride. In Newcastle, Max Lees was the leading jockey a decade before he trained the great Luskin Star to win the 1977 Golden Slipper. Billy Wade, the father of Luskin Star's jockey, Johnny Wade, was still riding then. Pat would catch the train up to Newcastle or head down to Kembla Grange with a book of four or five rides that kept his career momentum going.

Spider Webster had found work as a painter and docker on Garden Island where his reputation as a hard man was put to good use. He lived at the Glenmore Hotel at the Rocks and Pat would catch up with him regularly. 'One day I rode a double at Newcastle and Dad won a packet on it and slipped me a couple of hundred dollars.

'Pirate Lass was my first ride in a race in Sydney, at Canterbury Park, because I could ride so light – 6 stone 13 lbs (44kg). The same day I rode Count Remy for trainer Billy Wilson, carrying 9 stone 10 lb (62kg). I went from riding a 10 oz saddle in the first race to a 14 lb saddle because of the different weights the horses had to carry.'

Not long after, Pat had his first ride at Randwick on a horse called Medieval Maestro in the Henry Kendal Handicap. He had done well at the provincials, but how did he measure up at racing headquarters?

'In one of the closest finishes of the day,' wrote Ron Abbott in *The Sydney Morning Herald*, 'Medieval Maestro, ridden by former country apprentice Pat Webster, got up in the last stride to beat the heavily backed Somebody by a short half head. The favourite Aureo, was an unlucky third a head away'.

In a blanket finish, Abbott reported, 'apprentice Pat Webster had no doubt he had won on Medieval Maestro. He trotted him into the winner's stall without waiting for the judge to decide'. Jockeys are not allowed to enter the winner's stall until the winning number is semaphored and Pat was rebuked by steward Jack Burke for his haste. Pat had never ridden at Randwick before and didn't know what the protocol was. He then headed in the wrong direction for the weight in.

At 33/1, Medieval Maestro had snuck under the guard of most punters, ridden by a bush apprentice in a non-claiming race. The horse had drifted out under pressure, giving punters in the grandstand the illusion that Somebody had lasted to win on the fence. Somebody was backed from 8's to 11/2 and looked set to land some big bets.

'I wasn't very popular with punters', Pat laughs.

From there, the winners followed, even if the press were slow to get his name right. In a yellowed newspaper clipping in one of Pat's scrapbooks, a report dated 12 June 1967 states: 'Murky Night completed the hat-trick with a decisive win in the Entourage Handicap at Randwick today. Starting at the surprising good odds of 10/9, Murky Night was being eased down by his young rider Peter [sic] Webster at the finish.'

Pat also won on Singleton galloper Sky Sailor at 10/1 on the same card to pull off a rare Randwick double.

At least journalist Ken Calandra got his name right in *The Sun* the following week. 'Up and coming apprentice Pat Webster enhanced his claims as one of Sydney's most promising middle-distance riders when he won the Kurrajong Intermediate (9f) on Cisco Rose (9/2). Webster showed good judgement of pace to take the mare to the front soon after the start and led all the way.'

The winners started to come more frequently. Popular Choice won at 16/1 at Randwick, Pat rode Star Rise to victory for master Bernie Byrnes, and Miss Mink saluted as a 5/2 favourite at Canterbury. Star Rise won the Cannonby Stakes at Randwick after racing so wide Pat brought the gelding home underneath the judge's box. A tearaway win on Flagrant, sensationally backed from 12/1 to 4/s, ripped an estimated $50,000 from the betting ring.

Not that everything easily fell into place in Pat's riding career. He tumbled from Heroic Peak in a race at Rosehill and was taken to hospital for observation. Later, a flock of seagulls cost him victory at Rosehill when his mount Henderson took fright and veered off the track.

Pat was among the tallest jockeys in Sydney and battled weight problems like many of his competitors. 'I was always going to be a jockey so growing too big was not in my thinking.' But the issue was always in the back of his mind. When he was weighing out for a race, Pat formed the habit of leaning against the wall and slouching a little to appear smaller than the other jockeys.

The great Jack Thompson was said to be the tallest jockey in town, but Pat was taller still. '"Thommo" gave me a pair of his silks to wear one day and they didn't fit.' The teenager fell into bad habits, taking up smoking, popping pills and dieting excessively.

Duromine is one of the oldest diet pills in the market place. A prescription drug known in the sports business as 'legal speed', it is an appetite suppressant with an active ingredient called phentermine, which causes, among other symptoms, insomnia, nausea, headaches and an increased heart rate.

'I never came across pills before coming to the city. To be able to ride under 7 stone I had to stay slim … if you couldn't make the weight you couldn't take the ride. I'd take a Duromine at 4 am with a cup of coffee before doing trackwork, and then I would be able to go all day. But then I couldn't get to sleep at night. I'd still be lying there staring at the ceiling at two and three in the morning. Then the alarm would go off and I'd have to get up and take another pill and go off and do it all again … six days a week.'

On the morning of a race, Pat would take a couple of 'piss pills' to get rid of the fluid in his body in order to make the weight. 'It was entirely legal,' he says, 'and everyone was doing it. Nothing was going to stop me being a jockey. I just loved riding so much'.

Pat was starting to get noticed by the leading trainers too. 'I rode a winner for "TJ" one day, or Mr Smith I should say. Tommy put me on one of his horses in an "apprentices only" race, and it was very prestigious to ride for him … he was the man. Bart Cummings had no Sydney presence in those days, except at Carnival time when he brought a team up from Melbourne, but we became very close later in life when I turned to training.'

Pat also rode in a Doncaster Handicap (1600m) for Melbourne Cup-winning trainer Frank Lewis. 'I always wanted win a Doncaster as a jockey – not so much a Melbourne Cup or even the Golden Slipper', he says. 'To even have a mount in those big mile races was amazing.'

To racing purists like Pat, the Doncaster was one of the best races on the Australian racing calendar. Great horses like Chatham, Cabochon, Gunsynd, Tobin Bronze, Emancipation, Super Impose, Sunline and even the great Winx won Randwick's premier mile race. Half a century after first riding in the 'Donny,' Pat would win the race as the trainer of Happy Clapper … at his third try!

'The Doncaster is also one of the hardest races in Australia to win – there were a maximum twenty-four runners in those days all jockeying for position. They raced tighter than they do now and there were wooden running rails, not the flexible aluminium rails they have today, so the error of judgment was minuscule.'

It was nothing for an opposing jockey to buffet competitors into the running rail. 'You'd have to raise your right leg up so it wouldn't scrape along the running rail and break your ankle. There were no stewards' films around the back of the track in those days. Your iron would be scraping along the woodwork. Senior jockeys could get you into some awkward positions.'

Pat was a quick learner. 'Often, you'd let a jockey up your inside by half a length and then close the gap on them or give the horse a tap on the nose. Today you see jockeys going up the inside to win a race all the time, but in those days, you would never let a jockey get up underneath you. The running rail is always the quickest way home.'

Pat could outride the best of them too. 'I won a race on Clasp one day for high profile owner Jack Russo and I kept George Moore in a pocket for much of the straight. Moore was riding the favourite for Tommy Smith, and when he pulled up, Moore abused the shit out of me and said he was going to protest. He didn't have any grounds to protest, but he was Mr George Moore for Chrissake!

'A jockey named Keith Ashton rode past and said not to take any notice of Moore. "You just outrode him, son." When we got back to the jockey's room George was still blowing up about it.'

Pat later found out that George Moore had backed the mount and the last thing he expected was that a green kid from the bush would knock him off. 'But that's what happened', says Pat proudly.

Senior jockeys tried to get an edge over the young apprentices all the time, Pat says. 'I saluted on Popular Choice one day and the great George Moore ran second on a horse called El Hugo. It was well-known that Moore would ring around town and buy rides for his son Gary, and lo and behold, he rang Bernie Byrnes about securing the ride on Popular Choice.' Although Byrnes stuck solid with his apprentice, Moore got to the owners and Gary Moore was put on the horse.

'Gary had Popular Choice too handy, probably because they all backed it, and that didn't suit the horse. I hopped back on him next start and rode him the way he was trained, and he won at Randwick'.

Not that all jockeys were ruthless. 'Kevin Langby became a great friend', Pat says. 'I am godfather to his daughter, Sharon. Kevin was the leading jockey in Sydney at the time – a star – but he took me under his wing. He'd pick me up and take me to the races, and take me out to restaurants then bring me home. I also became very close to Ron Quinton, who was not only a champion jockey but a champion bloke. We would later become fellow trainers at Randwick, and are cast in the same mould, I think.'

Jockeys turned trainers … and Group 1-winning trainers at that.

'Jack Thompson was lovely man too. He gave me a pair of his riding boots; he was just so generous. And I realised just what a good horseman Darby McCarthy was riding against him. He borrowed my lead bag at Randwick when he won the AJC Derby on Divide and Rule and the Epsom on Broker's Tip on the same day. I was just happy to help out.'

In the autumn of 1969, Melbourne Cup winning trainer Frank Lewis used Pat's 5 lb allowance on his promising two-year-old Beau Babylon when it won by three lengths at Warwick Farm. 'I won three straight on Beau Babylon and retained the ride in the Golden Slipper, but we didn't know how good the Melbourne horse Vain was. Vain came around the outside of us and jockey Pat Hyland couldn't hold him.'

Vain won by four lengths. Pat finished down the track.

The Golden Slipper Stakes (1200m) was seen as showdown between Vain and the Sydney filly Special Girl, ridden by George Moore, but the Victorian champ made it a one-act affair. Lewis then took Pat off Beau Babylon in the Sires Produce (1400m) and replaced him with Victoria's premier jockey Roy Higgins. Beau Babylon caused the biggest boilover in a decade when he beat Vain by a half-length at 33/1.

'Sydney had a lot of rain before that race, and the trainer of Vain eased up on him, just trotting him around the middle of Randwick. Roy Higgins almost cut the horse in half to beat Vain – there no whip rules back then – but he was a champion jockey and the plain truth is the horse wouldn't have won with me on it. That made it a bit easier to handle but I don't mind admitting that I shed some tears when I lost the ride.'

Vain, the champion of his era, bounced back to with the third leg of the two-year-old triple crown, the Champagne Stakes (1600m) by a record ten lengths.

London Rep was Pat's last winner before the fall that would change his life in July 1969. Fittingly, London Rep was trained by Betty Lane and was backed from 100/1 to 12s when it led all the way at Canterbury. Bred by Narromine stud owner Les Gibson and owned by Gibson's wife, London Rep hadn't raced for almost two years before Lane set it for a first up win. Putting Pat on the horse was a great touch, but the country connection supported Lane's judgment by backing the horse off the map. The sting pulled an estimated $200,000 out of the betting ring at a time when the average median in house price in Sydney was $15,000.

'Bernie Byrnes said to me, "You'll get a good sling out of this son"'. I would see him standing anxiously at the letterbox waiting for the mail to come. When it did come, Bernie came in shaking his head. "It's only $50!" Even Tiger Holland was embarrassed.'

Pat's riding career came crashing down later that month in the last race at Rosehill. 'I was really firing at the time. It was a Saturday meeting and I had five rides, many of them favourites, but hadn't ridden a winner. I was riding a horse called Yarrandale – the only reason I got the ride was because a guy called Doug Spencer from Cowra trained it and he remembered me riding in the bush.'

Although he wouldn't have admitted it at the time, Pat was tired from wasting, and the pills affected his balance and concentration. 'It was a big field and I was running fourth or fifth.' Jockey Gary Rashley was on the outside of me, and Peter Miers on the inside. The gap opened up and when I took it, the horse clipped his heels and down I went.'

Pat says the mistake he made was trying to hang on to the horse. 'I panicked and I slipped under its neck. I knew it was a big field, with a lot of horses behind us, but it was my horse that did all the damage to me. We teach jockeys now to let go and roll … it may have been different if I'd done that. Even though some jockeys today don't like wearing the protective vests they use, it gives them a self-confidence when they hit the ground and provides protection to vital organs.' Pat didn't have that advantage back in 1969.

The teenager suffered a compound fracture of the leg, a shattered arm, fractured skull, broken ribs, busted pelvis and a broken collarbone. 'I was in hospital for several months and didn't ride for another nine months. I was transferred from Parramatta to St George hospital and was placed in a ward with a bunch of guys recovering from motorcycle accidents.'

Pat had ridden a horse called Get the Message in Newcastle which was owned by St George rugby league test stars Johnny Raper and Billy Smith. 'They travelled to Newcastle with me on the train but really, I had no idea who they were, not following league that closely. They backed the horse heavily each way one day when I rode it again at Randwick and it finished fourth. They had big hearts!'

When Pat was in St George hospital, Spider would visit him but he couldn't come every day because he had to work on the wharfs. 'My mate Kerry Pankhurst would catch three buses to come and see me, but the one person who came regularly was Johnny Raper. It just shows what a good bloke he is because he remembered me riding Get the Message and took the time to come and visit me. Sometimes he would bring Billy Smith and Graeme 'Chang' Langlands with him.'

Years later, Pat became good mates with the league legend, and his wife Carol, through his involvement with John Singleton. 'Singo once asked me to show "Chook" Raper how to ride a horse for a street parade. On the big day, "Chook" showed up in his best RM Williams gear and certainly looked the part. Nobody counted on someone in the crowd throwing fire crackers under the horse, however. "Chook" was thrown from the horse onto the asphalt.'

Pat slowly recovered from his injuries, but the compound fracture of his leg continued to cause him a lot of trouble. The doctors set it wrong when he was in hospital and then had to reset it. 'I put on a lot of weight in hospital and recuperating at the stables and all of a sudden I was a couple of stone heavier. I wasted heavily again and made it back to riding in races, but I couldn't keep my weight down.'

Increasing weight was limiting Pat's opportunities in the city so he decided to go back to Inverell and finish his apprenticeship with local trainer Bill Begley. Pat's last ride in Sydney was a sentimental one, on Ten-year-old Medieval Maestro, three years after he rode the horse to victory in his first race at Randwick. Although there was no fairy-tale win this time, Pat would find success in Inverell and renew old friendships.

'I always wanted to return home to Inverell and ride, to be a big fish in a little pond.' On New Year's Day, 1971, he rode a double at the local meeting. 'It was a great feeling, returning home a success.' He even renewed his friendship with Jack Dixon, often staying at the home of his childhood friend while he chased rides.

'It was as if Pat had come back to life', Jack remembers. 'We just took up from where we left off and have been mates ever since.'

But something, or more importantly, *someone* was drawing Pat back to the city.

CHAPTER 5

Chrissy's Story

Some years back, Christine 'Chrissy' Webster was at one of those AJC functions frequented by trainers, owners and the media, where some of Sydney's well-to-do like to hold the floor and talk about their favourite subjects … themselves. 'One committeeman was going on and on, boasting of his family's links to Governor Macquarie and the convict days, when he must have seen me roll my eyes or Pat nodding off', Chrissy says. 'After what seemed the longest time, he turned to me, no doubt noticing I am half Chinese, and asked, "and what's your background?"'

'Genghis Khan', Chrissy replied, quick as a flash. 'Thanks for asking.'

Christine Lee was actually born in Sydney into a Chinese-Irish family and raised in the Eastern Suburbs. Her father, Chinese immigrant Jimmy Lee, always told his children, 'the Lees weren't born rich but we were born lucky'.

And a lot of that luck rubbed off on Pat Webster when he married Chrissy. Her family's story is worthy of its own book.

The Lees' paternal grandfather was born in Mongolia, in Northern China, and was sold into servitude as a carpenter in New Guinea in the late 1930s. Chrissy's father Jimmy had been born in Canton in 1932, and the young family travelled to the nearest port, Honk Kong, on their way to their new life once the head of the family had set himself up there.

'My father says it took forever for him, his older sister Mary and Nanna Lee to get to New Guinea and join my grandfather', Chrissy says. The Lees did quite well there too, with Chrissy's grandfather opening a successful goods store.

When the Japanese invaded the island in 1942, shortly after the bombing of Pearl Harbour, ten-year-old Jimmy Lee and his family were evacuated to Sydney along with Australian nationals living in New Guinea. The Lees were resettled in Pyrmont, an inner-city suburb of Sydney, but they had left everything they owned back in New Guinea and had to start again.

Jimmy Lee went to school at Rozelle Christian Brothers. He played A-grade rugby league for the school but not before overcoming the racism of the times. 'I'm just a Chinaman', he would tell his kids when they asked him about his early life. 'When I went to school, I was the only Chinaman and there was only one other Greek boy there.' Faced with naked racism from a fellow student, his solution was simple and immediately effective.

Jimmy belted the crap out of him.

Jimmy Lee may have felt like an outsider, but he was well-educated, smart and hard-working. Before long, the Lees opened up a fruit shop, leased several storage warehouses and operated a taxi business. 'Dad often said, thank God the federal government after World War II let the "refos" stay in the country', Chrissy remembers. Despite welcoming the birth of two more daughters in Australia, the White Australia Policy was still in operation and Jimmy's parents feared they would be deported back to China at any moment.

Jimmy Lee met his future wife, Patricia Nellie Wallis, a North Sydney Catholic girl with blonde hair with green eyes, in the early 1950s. The fact that her family didn't accept Jimmy didn't deter Tootie, as she was known, one bit. 'I can't imagine what they went through', Chrissy says, alluding to a time when interracial marriages were not the norm. 'But we were survivors. First child James was born in 1954, followed by Greg, me, David, Wayne and my beautiful sister Sharon.'

The Lees lived at Five Dock originally before moving next door to their Chinese grandparents at Randwick. 'Sons are always important in

Chinese culture,' Chrissy explains, 'and my grandfather (or 'gong gong' in Cantonese) wanted Dad near him'. They grew up in a happy, extended family setting.

'We were happy because we had each other', Chrissy says. 'Our Chinese grandparents could barely speak English, but they were beautiful, simple people. They lived in the Eastern Suburbs but they had yard chickens and would cut the heads off in their back yard and prepare most of their own food. They even took one of Greg's phantom pigeons and made a pie out of it.'

Jimmy Lee and his young family also lived with Tootie's family for a time. 'My Australian grandfather was an SP bookie who drove a big Pontiac. When he took me to the shops, he would spoil me and buy me three pairs of shoes. We grew up surrounded by music – my grandmother played the piano, and there was always music in the house.'

The Lees enjoyed the best of both families, Chinese and Australian, although the two rarely mixed. Jimmy was a Buddhist, but Chrissy's mother was Catholic and raised her children in the Catholic tradition 'with a Buddhist leaning from dad', Chrissy says.

'Tootie would take us kids for a walk to the shops,' Chrissy remembers, 'and people would think she was a nanny. "Whose children are these?" people would ask. "They're all mine", she would say proudly before walking on'. Chrissy says her mother stood out with her 1960s, blonde beehive hairdo and a tribe of half-Chinese children but she never took a backward step in her life.

'Mum had long arms that were always wrapped around us', Chrissy says with pride. 'But our father was not allowed to speak Chinese to us in front of my mother', she concedes. '"They're flat out speaking English," Tootie would say, "don't confuse them". As a result, we could understand a few Chinese words but not a lot.'

The oldest Lee brothers, Jim and Greg, became apprentice jockeys, as did younger brother David, despite the fact they had not been brought up around horses. 'They were just small,' Chrissy says, 'and because Jim and Greg were so close in age many people thought they were twins'. The Lee brothers became successful jockeys in their own right and were apprenticed to trainer Cec Rowles before linking with the Les Bridge stable.

'They rode a lot of winners for TJ Smith too', Pat interrupts. 'Cec only had a couple of horses in work so they had plenty of time to ride for other trainers.'

Pat Webster first met the Lee brothers riding trackwork at Randwick. He was an established apprentice jockey and a couple of years older than them so they called him 'Mr Webster' when they crossed paths. 'Don't call me Mr Webster', he would tell them. Pat was still a teenager himself.

At an early stage of their career, Pat and Jim Lee found themselves going to the Hawkesbury barrier trials in the back of a float. 'We were riding in the float holding onto the horses – no seat belts or anything, just bouncing around the back', Pat says. 'We went under an overhead bridge and we heard bolts scraping through the float roof. When we got out, the float was stuck under the bridge and we couldn't get the horses out of the float. I went across the road to a corner shop and brought Jim a soft drink while they let the tyres down to lower the float.'

That one act of kindness, Pat shouting young Jim a Coke at a time when money was hard to come by, endeared 'Mr Webster' to the Lee family before they even met him.

'My mate Kerry Pankhurst and me were getting too heavy and not getting rides. Having turned eighteen, we went off to Coogee for a beer at the Coogee Bay Hotel and a swim. We were so poor we couldn't afford swimmers so we wore cut down jeans. There was a dance promotion on stage on the beach with surf music blaring and I could see a tiny, black-haired lass in a red bikini doing "The Stomp". I said to Kerry, "What a good sort she is", and he said not to worry about that. "You'll never get to meet her", he told me.'

Pat was riding trackwork one morning when Greg Lee called out to him. 'Mr Webster! We're having a card game tonight at our house. Would you like to come?'

'Greg gave me an address and Chrissy answered the door.' The teenager dancing on the beach was the Lees' younger sister. 'The next day I told Kerry, remember the stomper in the bikini we saw at the beach last week? Well, I met her last night.'

'I had "jigged" school with a girlfriend to take part in the dance competition', Chrissy laughs. 'We had our uniforms in our carry bags.' The girls were caught out, confessed to their plan and summarily punished. 'It just goes to show I wouldn't have made a good thief.'

Pat was smitten; he asked Jimmy Lee if he could take his daughter out on a date. Chrissy was only a teenager, and he thought this was the polite thing to do. 'Jimmy said, "what are you asking me for? Ask her!"'

The close-knit Lee family somehow let the shy bush kid into the fold. 'Just', Chrissy says. Pat opened up with stories about what happened to him over the years ... the death of his mother, having to fend for himself from a young age and his recent fall. 'Dad was standoffish at first but he could see Pat was a good person. Mum saw straight away that he had done it hard in life.'

'There's a lot more to that boy', Chrissy's mum would say, sizing up the teenager.

When Pat went to Inverell to ride in the last year of his apprenticeship, he continued a long-distance relationship with Chrissy before returning to Sydney in the middle of 1971. It was about this time Chrissy had the difficult conversation with her mother most teenagers seek to avoid. 'You're not going to believe what happened', Chrissy remembers saying to her mother.

Chrissy was pregnant. 'Mum just looked at me, and then said to Pat, "Well, you should know better". She then asked me stay behind so she could talk to me. I will never tell anyone what she said to me, but Mum was wonderful and after that I knew what I wanted to do.

Having just turned twenty-one, Pat married Chrissy in 1972. Trainer Betty Lane had built a second house on her property in Geurie and offered Pat accommodation and a retainer to become her stable jockey again, but he would have to lose a lot of weight to resume his riding career. Chrissy says, 'I've never seen anything so horrifying in my life … the wasting he did! But at least I knew he had the self-discipline to achieve what he wanted to do'.

'Tiger Holland came to our flat in Bray Street, Bronte, and talked me into coming back to Geurie. But when I got up there, Betty didn't want to pay me the retainer we had agreed to and, although we had some success – I won the Gilgandra Cup, I recall – after six months I went back to Sydney to find work.' Chrissy, heavily pregnant, joined him soon after and son Patrick was born in Sydney.

'Chrissy's dad went halves with us and we bought a unit in Rose Bay. We lived in a one-bedroom apartment in Cook Road, with a kerosene heater for warmth, but that gave us a start on the real estate ladder. Later we brought a house in Clovelly with Chrissy's dad again going halves with us.'

Chrissy didn't meet Pat's family until some years later. 'I didn't even know he had two sisters until much later, but Lesley and Fay were lovely', Chrissy remembers. 'They were fountains of knowledge about Pat's family and helped fill in a lot of gaps.' The greatest compliment they paid Chrissy, she says, was when they said to her, 'Mum would have adored you, the way you look after *"The Baby"*. They still called Pat that'.

Pat's father Spider was a tougher nut to crack. 'Oh, no, you're "Chinee"', he blurted out when he met Chrissy for the first time. 'There's an "s" on the end of that, mate', Chrissy corrected him. 'It's "Chinese", not "Chinee".'

But Chrissy won Spider over too. 'Spider lived with us in the last years of his life', Chrissy says. 'Pat was so busy as a trainer I saw more of Spider than I did of my own husband during those years. Spider was so proud of our son, Patrick … all three kids could run a bit and were good at sport and he would say to anyone who was listening, "Come and watch my grandchildren run".'

'When Wayne was born, I woke Spider up in the middle of the night and said, "Pop, I have a pain … the baby's coming".

'"Don't tell me now', he replies, 'it's still too dark".'

Chrissy nursed Spider in his final years after he contracted cancer. 'Pop knew he was dying of cancer, having been a smoker all his life', she says. 'When he was living with us, he said, "Before I leave this earth I'm going to teach you how to cheat at cards". Towards the end of his life, I would accuse him of cheating at euchre and he'd say, "Well, you are too!"'

'Pat's father had a colourful life, but he was also a gentleman', says Chrissy. 'He was always immaculately dressed and he never swore in front of a woman.' When he passed away in 1984, the family buried Spider alongside his beloved wife Blanche in Dubbo. Chrissy's name is also on the gravestone as a mark of respect for what she did for him when he was sick.

'Chrissy was amazing', Pat says. 'She was more than just a daughter-in-law to him.'

Chrissy also helped nurse her own mother during her final years when Alzheimer's disease took her about five years ago. 'She was a wonderful mother and just so resilient. If we complained about anything when we were kids, she would look at us and say, "Are you serious? What do you have to complain about?"'

Pat Webster is a self-made man, building his stable and reputation from scratch, and he's worked hard for that. But he's also had a good, strong woman in his corner. At the beginning of his training career, Pat admits he felt inferior to the bigger Randwick stables with their better-bred horses and millionaire owners, but Chrissy put it all in perspective for him.

'Pat, they're just horse trainers like you', she'd tell him. 'But your story is so much more interesting.

'Those trainers went to private school to learn how to train. Pat rode a pony to school to learn his trade.'

Chrissy Webster not only became Pat's wife and partner, but also his sternest defender.

'In the 1980s, I was training a horse for John Singleton which dead-heated one day in a race somewhere. I actually protested after the race but when the stewards asked how much the alleged interference had cost my horse, I thought I'd be smart and say half a head when I should have said half a length. The protest was dismissed.'

Singo was working at Radio 2KY at the time and couldn't be at the races. There were no mobile phones back then, of course, and the only chance I got to talk to Singo after the race was back home when I was taking a bath. Chrissy handed me the extension phone and Singo gave me an almighty spray about how the horse should have won. And it had dead-heated for first!'

When he handed the phone back to Chrissy, she asked what the high-profile owner wanted and Pat said, somewhat off-handedly, that the call was just to abuse him about how he trained the horse. 'Chrissy fires up and says that I didn't need that aggravation and that she was going to ring him back. "He can't say that to you." I think Singo owned three of the eight horses in my stable, but she told him we would send the horses back to him on a livestock float the next day.'

Chrissy organised for the horses to leave the stable the following morning. Singo was living at Vaucluse at the time, which was the only address the stable had, and when he came out onto his driveway in his bathrobe, there were three horses waiting for him on a float. He ended up sending them to Princess Farm, in Castlereagh, which he owned before selling the property to Bart Cummings.

'The next time he saw me,' Pat continues, 'Singo says, "You can call off Fighting Harada, now". He couldn't even get that right; Chrissy is half Chinese, not Japanese, but she took it her stride. Singo still calls Chrissy

"Fighting", for short'.

And it certainly didn't mean the end of the Websters' friendship with the high profile, much-married ad-man. 'We've been great mates ever since', Singleton says. 'Fair enough returning horses if the owner is being a dickhead. I had the same attitude in advertising ... if a client was being difficult or rude to my staff, they were soon gone, even if I couldn't afford to lose them at the time'.

'Singo gave me a horse to train recently called King Billy', Pat says. 'He lives up here on the Central Coast and I like his company, so I called around to have lunch with him and Chrissy picked me up. When he was walking me to the car he said to Chrissy, "I wish I had something like you and Pat have, maybe I'd still be married".'

'Chrissy shot back, "Money can't buy that mate". Singo laughed too, because he learnt long ago not to argue with Chrissy.'

'Would Pat have been as successful as he is without "Fighting Harada" by his side?' Singo asks himself when Pat and I catch up with him for coffee near his Central Coast home. 'I don't think so. Chrissy is Pat's rock, in good times and bad.'

A couple of years ago, just after Happy Clapper won the 2015 Villiers Stakes, Pat and Chrissy had to call on their reserves of resilience when youngest son Wayne was diagnosed with cancer of the lymph glands. 'Wayne found a lump on the side of his head after having a haircut', Chrissy explains. 'Pat said to him, "Mate, you need to go straight to the doctors and see about that". Both of Pat's parents died of cancer, so he didn't muck around.'

It was a scary time for the wider Webster clan; Wayne and his wife had two young daughters and were trying for a third. When Wayne awoke from his operation to remove the cancerous lymph glands, his first question was, 'How did Happy Clapper go in the Bill Ritchie Handicap?'

Wayne is now cancer free, and has recently lost 40kg after medication sent his weight soaring. Before his chemotherapy, he had his sperm frozen in case he couldn't have any children. Since then Wayne and his wife Lee have welcomed two more children into the family, including a son they named Patrick James Webster.

The torch has been passed on.

Recently Pat decided to take Chrissy back to his hometown of Inverell. 'There was a race meeting there with some young apprentices I wanted to talk to too and although it was out of my area, Keith Bullock from Racing NSW agreed that I could go up there in my role as a mentor. I took Chrissy along to show her some of my local haunts.'

It had been more than fifty years since Pat Webster had left his hometown of Inverell. He and Chrissy visited his family home, caught up with old friend Jack Dixon and his wife and attended the race meeting in town. On the way back to Sydney, they stopped off in Dubbo, and saw the garage where he lived with other apprentices at Trevor Wrigley's farm in the 1960s. The shed was old, but still standing, although the Wrigleys were long gone. The Websters also visited the graves of Pat's mother and father.

It has been a long and successful journey together for Pat and Chrissy Webster.

'We worked together as a team and made a good life for ourselves and our kids', Chrissy says. 'It hasn't always been easy, but it's always been good.'

CHAPTER 6

Painters and Dockers

The Federated Ship Painters and Dockers Union (FSPDU), colloquially known as the 'Painters and Dockers' was one of the country's most notorious trade unions. Before it was officially deregistered in 1993, a decade after the findings of the Costigan Royal Commission (1980), the Painters and Dockers – more so in Melbourne than Sydney or Newcastle – were condemned as a front for criminal enterprise and tax evasion. The infamous dockland wars of the 1970s and 1980s resulted in the murders of at least fifteen people, including FSPDU Secretary Pat Shannon who was gunned down in a Melbourne pub in 1973.

Originally, workers on the nation's wharfs were involved in a wide variety of jobs – 'chipping, painting, scrubbing [and] cleaning [ships], working in every size of tanks, cleaning boilers, docking and undocking vessels, and rigging work'. But as the manual work on the docks became increasingly mechanised in the 1960s and 1970s, the increasingly militant Painters and Dockers Union attempted to maintain control its controversial 'roster' system that had been in operation since the end of the War with a series of rolling strikes in the 1970s and 1980s.

The 'roster' system protected branch offices in each port in the allocation of wharf jobs to union members. It was against this backdrop former apprentice jockey Pat Webster became a painter and docker in the early 1970s.

'Spider was a rigger at Cockatoo Island, and I needed a job when I came back to Sydney, so he asked me if I wanted to be a rigger there too'.

Pat's father was second in charge at the Balmain 'hiring hall' at 36 Mort Street. What followed, according to Pat, were the most interesting years of his life.

***

When Pat's time as a jockey at Geurie turned sour, he returned to Sydney and 'fell into' a job selling advertising at *The Australian* for News Limited. For a kid who left school at age thirteen, and who admits he couldn't spell to save himself, it was a daunting task. But with a baby on the way, Pat was up for anything.

'I would pick a real estate advert out of the *Sun Herald* and then ring the customer and tell them I could double the size of the ad for the same price, maybe less', Pat says.

At lunchtime, when the journos when to the pub, Pat would man the phones and field incoming calls recording death notices. Being a poor speller, he would use a tape recorder attached to the phone to record the names of the customers, 'which were sometimes impossible to spell,' he says, 'so I would ask them to "please spell the name" just to be sure'. He would then give the recording to one of the girls in the typing pool to transcribe.

Pat worked for News Ltd for about twelve months before becoming a rigger on Sydney's docks, lifting and moving heavy objects on ships with chain hoists and cranes. But first he had to join the infamous 'Painters and Dockers' union.

'Before you could work on the docks, you had to go to the Quarterly Union meeting at the Town Hall and "walk the floor".' The union leadership would sit behind a large desk up the front with the members seated on both sides of the floor. If any member said they saw you in the company of police, they could call out and challenge your membership. Half of them would be pissed, so anything could happen.'

Pat was just twenty-two years old. 'Of course, I started walking across the floor and the members all knew my father was Spider and they started calling out, "Nah, not him …" The union leader got to his feet and yelled, "Now shut the fuck up!" and that was that'. He was in.

Pat's first day as a painter and docker certainly lived up to the reputation. 'I arrived at the Union Hall in Mort Street, Balmain, at 7.30 am for the daily call-out. Most of the guys were playing cards while they waited for their numbers to be called out. Tommy Fox was calling out the jobs. He was a thorough gentleman, so I don't know how in the hell he became a painter and docker.'

'All of a sudden, a bloke comes barging into the room carrying a handgun. He spots a guy sitting at a table and calls out, "You bastard!" and fires two shots at him that miss. The other guy bolted out the back door, with the bloke with the gun in hot pursuit.'

When the man with the gun burst through the door, Pat's father Spider pushed him to the ground and laid on top of him. 'When we got up and went out the back door to see what happened, both blokes were gone but there was a bullet hole in the gravity water tank with water pouring out of it.'

It was almost too much for young Pat. 'I said to Dad, "Fuck this for a job!" He later downplayed the incident, dismissing it as a domestic dispute between the two men, which had nothing to do with criminals. "Stick it out, son, the job will make a man out of you".'

'The funny thing is,' Pat says as he tells the story, 'I can still remember the gun the guy fired. It was a Luger pistol like the Germans soldiers had in World War II movies'.

Pat threw himself into the work, and admits there was a little bit of an ego about being 'a painter and docker' at the time. 'I now realise that Spider was employed there not because he was a good rigger, but because he was a good "knuckle man". His job was not only to keep the men who worked there in line, but also stop criminal groups getting out of hand.'

Pat stayed in the job for about five years. 'And I still have my have my roster book, too. No.600.'

Each worker's roster book would be placed on a large board in ten rows, starting at the bottom and slowly move their way up to the top row as the work came in. 'After picking up a day's work, your number would go back on the board at the same position. When the daily jobs came through, you'd hope they'd get to your number.'

Pat says that you would never take a job that was more than two days long because you would lose your place on the board and go down to the bottom. 'If the jobs were any longer, say a four-week stint on Garden Island, you'd "snatch it" and wait for another job. That job would then go to a bloke who may have needed the work at that time and could afford to lose his place on the board.'

The highest position Pat got on the board was No.9, with a little help and guidance from Spider. 'Some blokes worked on the docks for twenty years and never made the top ten.'

Pat worked mostly on a floating crane called the Titan, which was the largest in the southern hemisphere. 'It was fucking huge!' Pat says, his eyes widening on the last word. 'Tugs would tow the crane down from Cockatoo Island to White Bay, anchor it in the harbour and it would lift ships up out of the water.

'It was hard work, but a lot of good fun.'

Pat used to climb right up to the top of the Titan crane as it went under the Sydney Harbour Bridge. 'You'd swear blind you were going to hit the Bridge as you went underneath it.'

In 1991, after the Cockatoo Island dockyards closed, the crane was sent to Singapore despite being heritage-listed. It was being towed there when it suddenly collapsed on Christmas Eve and had to be scuttled.

'Before I could be a rigger on the wharves, I had to do night school to learn the breaking strength of certain widths of wire and the rest of it. I was better than anyone in splicing wire, but in a written test I might get 15 out of 100.' It is a credit to Pat that with very little schooling behind him, he stuck with his studies and achieved the certificates he needed. 'I never even went to high school, so it was all fairly new to me', he says.

There was a turf war going on at the Melbourne docks at the time, which had more to do with criminality than the nature of the work. 'A lot of guys escaped the wars by heading north and working up here under "bodgie" names', Pat says. 'There were no tax file numbers back then and guys could work under any name they wanted. They would come up to Sydney for a couple of weeks while the smoke cleared and then return to Melbourne.'

The Sydney docks were different to the war-torn Melbourne shipyards, Pat says, and the union didn't want criminal elements from down south working up here. 'That's where Spider and the union reps came in.'

'But that's not to say everything was above board here is Sydney', Pat says. 'I was working on the submarines at Cockatoo Island – there was no place to hide working in such a confined place so we got the job done – but when a ship came in, it would dry dock and guys would scrub the barnacles off the hull and paint it. There wasn't a lot of work going on, really. Blokes took their time.'

Pat recalls there was a guy on the docks named 'Gunboat' who took the orders for the workers' lunches. 'He used to drink a bottle of Listerine out of a paper bag on the ferry to work, for the alcohol content. Workers would tell him they were being laid off and they couldn't afford to be.'

'You'll have to go on workers "compo",' Gunboat would tell them.

'Gunboat had this big square wooden mallet and when he pulled it out, he'd say, "This won't hurt much", which was probably a lie. He'd give the poor guy two painkillers and tell him to wash them down with a bottle of sweet musket cherry wine. Then he would smash the guy's finger with the mallet.'

A doctor in leafy Woollahra did all the worker's compensation for the painters and dockers, Pat says. 'I was told that the doctor's father had been ripped off by some insurance company and this was his way of paying them back.' The worker with the smashed finger would be placed on four weeks' leave.

Spider Webster later bought the lease on the Australian Hotel in the Rocks with a lady he befriended named Joyce. 'He had a quid by then and all the painters and dockers drank there in Cumberland Street.' Spider did that for three years, but the work almost killed him. 'It was hard work,' Pat says, 'and the temptation was that he would become his best customer. Everyone wanted to have a drink with him'.

The recession hit Australia hard in the mid-1970s, especially on the docks. Living in a 'one-bedder' behind the SCG in Paddington with baby Patrick was a real struggle for the family, and then daughter Diane arrived in 1975 with another one on the way (youngest son Wayne was born in 1978).

Pat finally left the docks behind, he says, because there was no job security. 'The mateship was great,' Pat says, 'but the docks were changing, with new systems coming in, so I could see the writing on the wall'.

Father-in-law Jimmy Lee had secured Pat a second job at the BP Aquatic service station in fashionable Rose Bay, but the family were still struggling to make ends meet so Pat got a job at Ansett Airport as a porter. 'Because of my country upbringing, I was used to hard work so I accepted all the overtime they threw at me', Pat says. He was often working double shifts until late at night but paying a lot of money in tax.

Working at Ansett and BP, Pat threw a third job into the mix when he went back to Randwick looking for trackwork. When he worked on the docks, Pat left his old life at the track behind him, never having a bet or walking onto a racecourse. 'Even when I was working at Ansett and was riding trackwork at Randwick, guys would ask me for a tip and I would say to them, "Boys, I couldn't tell you what was running". I had no interest in them.'

The reason was simple. 'I worked too hard to earn the money I did without losing it on the punt', he adds. 'It's probably the Scottish in me – being too mean – but I'm also not a good loser.'

Pat was still only about 60kg and riding horses was second nature to him, but rackwork was hard to get in those days, he says, especially at Randwick. Pat had ridden tearaway leader Pirate Bird for Pat Murray as an apprentice jockey and the Randwick trainer gave him a go.

'Pat Murray was a lovely, kind and friendly man, with a touch of eccentricity, but try getting $40 wages out of him on Saturday before a race day', Pat laughs.

Pat was sitting at the Rusty Shovel at Kensington having a beer after another exhausting week when he told wife Chrissy he was going to have a go at training horses. 'We're just paying too much in tax', he told her. He remembers Chrissy saying, 'If you take out a trainer's licence that will solve our tax problem because we might not earn enough money to even pay tax.'

'There were people pulling off some big plunges in Sydney at the time and I thought if these guys can do that, then I could too', Pat says. Although he was not a punter, he was confident in his own ability as a horseman and that he could attract owners and stable punters who shared this faith.

And Chrissy agreed with Pat. 'I always believed you should do what you're best at, and for Pat that was working with horses. Pat knew horses.'

While he waited for the AJC to grant him a trainer's licence, Pat took on the foreman's role of his former master, Bernie Byrnes. He could have done that for a career without the stress of running his own stable, but the wages just weren't good enough for a young man with three young children. More importantly, Pat was ready to be his own boss.

'The licensing steward at Randwick was a guy called Ryan. I was told by another trainer when I went in for the interview to start asking about the steward's health. "He'll start talking about how sick he is and if you sit there listening to him for an hour, you've a chance of getting a licence".'

Pat was a good listener and was granted a provisional trainer's licence.

In 1978, Pat Webster was probably the youngest trainer at Randwick. As a jockey, he had always been told that he wouldn't hit his prime until his late 20s. At age twenty-seven, he was starting out in racing all over again and it would take him considerably longer to his hit his prime as a horse trainer.

CHAPTER 7

A Trainer's Life

In 1978, noted Sydney racing scribe Bert Lillye offered the following titbit in his regular Friday column:

> **The face was familiar but it did not match the figure. This tricked me when I saw Pat Webster at Newmarket last week ...**
>
> **'You don't know me, do you?' Webster said when he introduced himself.**
>
> **Webster, 27, wants to get back into racing. He has applied to the AJC for a trainer's licence and he has been promised a two-year-old filly from New Zealand.**

The problem remained. Pat had no stables, no staff and no horses. 'There were no training boxes on course at Randwick at the time', Pat says. 'They were all privately owned on properties in the local area. I was told if I could find boxes near Randwick, I'd be granted a licence.'

Chrissy's brothers, Jim and Greg Lee, were coming to the end of their riding careers and were also considering a move into training. 'Their dad bought six stables on the corner of South Dowling Street. Greg knew an ex-Detective named Frank Amanasco who worked for Mrs Kath Munro, the widow of champion jockey 'Darby' Monro. Mrs Munro owned eight boxes on Doncaster Avenue and Frank recommended me to her. That's how I started training.'

Pat was always thankful to his brothers-in-law for securing him stable accommodation. 'They could have grabbed the stables for themselves', he says. 'They had to float their horses from their stables to Randwick for trackwork, which I felt really bad about. If I had a couple of horses overflow that were injured or needed vet assistance, I would keep them down at the Lees' stable because that helped them out too.' David Lee later became a trackwork rider for Pat, while Jim and Greg Lee also rode for him when they were available.

The two-year-old filly from New Zealand Pat was promised was called Young Sally. 'David knew a guy called Tony Porter at Oakdale. He gave me my first horse to lease, which was Young Sally, and he was a very loyal owner for me over the years.'

Graeme Rogerson previously trained Young Sally in New Zealand, and although she was still a maiden when Pat secured her, the filly had untapped potential. 'I was so excited to get my first horse that I went to meet Young Sally when she arrived at the airport. She looked good, but then the guy leading her out gave me three photos of her winning races over the carnival at Poverty Bay.'

'What's this?' Pat asked. Perhaps knowing he was losing the horse, Rogerson kept backing the filly up and she just kept winning. 'I was in the ownership along with a couple of knockabouts I knew at the Charing Cross Hotel and now she couldn't race in maiden company, obviously. She won a couple of races for us but was terribly unlucky.'

Young Sally had a heartbreaking run of five seconds and three thirds before winning at Hawkesbury, but all this did was make Pat more determined to succeed. Tony Porter also gave Pat the filly Misty Love, which was beaten by a head in the 1979 Summer Cup, and another called Kiss of Gold. 'Tony really got me going', he says.

Pat chose orange with a black Maltese Cross and hoops as his stable colours. He originally chose green as the main colour, but his father Spider said green was unlucky because he had never won on a horse carrying those colours.

'I was driving along Allison Road to the AJC offices to register my colours when the lights changed from green to orange to red. I thought to myself that the powers that be must have put a lot of research into why those colours are so recognisable, so with Spider's words ringing in my ears, I changed the colours from green to orange.'

The Maltese cross was pretty much the only motif the AJC allowed on jockey's silks in those days, he says. 'Unlike today, where you can have a dolphin, a car or a picture of your mother on the silks.'

Pat had a good strike rate for a small trainer but, not surprisingly, the winners just didn't come often enough in the early years. He describes himself as being 'pretty lucky' as a trainer, but that was mainly through hard work. Up at 3 am on most mornings, it was a backbreaking routine for small reward.

'And I did most of the work myself', Pat says. 'I learned at an early age how to care for horses – I could do everything but shoe them. At a stretch, I could hammer a tack in but I could certainly take them off!'

Stable hand Noel Fulmer was also a great help in those early years, Pat says. 'We'd walk the horses across Doncaster Avenue two at a time and he'd ride half of them and I'd ride the others in the early hours of the morning.'

Pat also had the service of apprentice riders Johnny Hay and Craig Hyeronimus. 'Craig finished up champions apprentice jockey of his year and is the father of jockey Adam Hyeronimus. Johnny Hay couldn't get a ride with TJ Smith so he came over to me. When he got too heavy, he became my track rider.' Tragically, Hay later died of a drug overdose.

Being a trainer who could ride his own trackwork was also a huge advantage, Pat says. 'I could be riding a horse in work and decide to give her a little more or bring her back underneath me according to how it felt and how track conditions were.' It also gave him an insider's knowledge when a horse was ready to win. Not that everything always went to plan.

Pat's first winner in the city was Silver Ketch, ridden by apprentice jockey Malcolm Johnstone, starting at the unbelievable odds of 250/1. The only problem was, no one backed it.

'I always had a good relationship with Malcolm's master, Theo Green, and he never played favourites with his jockeys. He allocated his jockeys to the first rides that were offered them and we got in early with Malcolm, who was winning on everything at the time, although it was unusual for him to ride such a roughie.'

Silver Ketch was entered in a midweek race at Canterbury, and was going really well on the track when she suffered an attack of colic. 'When a horse got colic in those days, you filled them up with oil so they got really soft inside and they could pass their droppings', Pat explains. 'The vet said she would be ok to run – she had overcome her bout of colic – and I found out later that the breed (by Royal Yacht) had to be kept fresh so it suited her not to do any work leading up to the race.'

Silver Ketch was near last on the turn, but Malcolm Johnstone zigzagged his way through a big field and saluted at cricket score odds. 'We were going to back her, but after the colic, we didn't have a cent on it', Pat laments.

Pat then received the news that would change his fortunes overnight. Frank Amanasco rang him, and in his slow, dry delivery, informed him that Kath Munro wanted to transfer several horses she had with TJ Smith to his stable … right away. The best of these was Marlborough, a high-priced, $40,000 son of boom New Zealand sire Oncidium which had been a costly failure at his previous start as a 7/4 favourite.

'The thought of taking Marlborough off TJ was daunting, but the Lord was looking down on me and he won his first three races in my stable. Smith's Tulloch Lodge was only a couple of blocks away and the next minute the horse was in my yard. That was on the Friday, and Marlborough won for me the next day at Randwick over 2000m'.

Confidently handled by Gavin Duffy, Marlborough gave Pat his first Saturday winner in town. 'I've taken him to the beach a couple of times and the salt water seems to have done him the world of good', the young trainer told pressmen keen to follow up on the story of the former apprentice jockey-turned-trainer.

'We had sneaked Marlborough into the 1979 Melbourne Cup with just 47.5kg, but he wasn't a sound horse and he suffered a bone chip on a fetlock later in his preparation', Pat says. The plan was always to leave the horse in Melbourne with noted Cup-winning trainer George Hanlon, Pat admits, so he didn't mind losing his 'good' horse. Marlborough later ran third in the 1980 Sydney Cup behind the champions Kingston Town and Double Century at the juicy odds of 200/1.

'George Hanlon was a great trainer, and he use to stable his horses with Bernie Byrnes when he was in Sydney', Pat says. 'I always thought that if I was going to style myself on another trainer, it would be George. He was so patient and kind with his horses. Other trainers tended to gallop their horses too much but George was a "pacework" man, slowly building the distances his horses raced. He had great success in the Melbourne Cup with Piping Lane (1972), Arwon (1978) and later Black Knight (1984), so why not follow his lead?'

As a result, Pat still keeps the trackwork light for the horses in his stable, even a champion like Happy Clapper. 'Treat your horses like babies and look after them, and they'll look after you.'

Hanlon was a character – a 'one-off' Pat says – but he could be very forgetful. 'He was in another world, really', Pat laughs. Hanlon would change a rug on a horse three times a day, forgetting that he had already done it. 'Once, when checking a horse, he misplaced a thermometer and had to clean out the entire stall lest the horse ate it.'

Pat was unafraid to try something different, and he was keen to learn from the best. 'A lot of senior trainers were a lot older than me, and I was no threat at all to them so we got along great. I just flew under the radar.'

Theo Green was another training legend Pat got close to. 'I was good mates with Theo's foreman Kenny Stone when I was an apprentice jockey', Pat says. 'Theo always stood on "Half Mile Hill" watching his horses and I got to talking to him over the years. "Hello Mr Green" … I was always very polite.'

Years later when Bart Cummings opened a stable at Randwick, Pat sought the company of the 'Cup Kings'. 'Bart and TJ Smith had an understanding', Pat says. 'Bart was the King of Melbourne racing but TJ was King of Sydney.'

'Bart used to come out to trackwork in the morning always eating an apple. I used to sit down beside him and engage with him, hoping to learn something from "The Master".' Bart was the best feeder in racing, Pat says. 'Old-time trainers like Bart and George Hanlon fed their horses lots of oats and corn. Now, it's all pre-mixed feeds, but I still add corn to my feed bins.'

Pat stayed with Mrs Munro's stables for several years until the AJC started building pre-fab boxes at Randwick. 'I applied for boxes on track and was surprised when I was allocated six. Since then, I've had two stables backing on to the course on Doncaster Avenue, but I'm back on track now in the same stables I started off in all those years ago.'

Pat also operated a hard and fast rule that if a horse was not up to scratch, he would tell the owners straight up. 'It's not worth the man hours to train it', a young and hungry trainer told journalist Glenn Robbins at the time. 'It's not fair to myself nor the owners paying the bills. Having a horse in training is not cheap, so owners are better off dispersing with the slow ones and getting a replacement who might be faster.'

And he could be brutally honest with his owners. Once, John Singleton sent Pat a well-bred horse and rang to see what the trainer thought of it. 'Well, it arrived in the horse ambulance', Pat joked. 'It looks like someone turned it upside down and stuck its legs on backwards.'

Pat would send those horses not up to city class to his mate Jack Dixon to race in Inverell, or up to Johnny Quinlan, the former apprentice jockey who was then training at Mudgee, where they were more likely to win a race.

'Even then, some owners didn't like to be told their horse was no good', he says. 'Three years later they'd ring me and tell me I was wrong. They've just won a maiden at Port Macquarie or somewhere and I'd think, "Fuck me … it only cost them another $50,000 to prove me wrong".'

But slowly the stable hits its straps, and when everything came together there was more than enough money to go around. A horse called Revelsar won three races in the early 1980s for connections, including an estimated $50,000 in one sting for popular owner Ron Callaghan, when it was ridden by Ron Quinton. Pat's sling enabled him to pay off a huge chunk of his mortgage on the family home in Clovelly.

'Ronnie loved a punt and was very generous', Pat says. 'He was known as "Lord Nuffield" to his mates because when he had a winner, he would shout the bar and then take us all out to dinner to the best Chinese restaurant in Cronulla. The next day we would follow up with a lobster BBQ at the stables for my staff.'

Pat had a horse called Paris Kiss in at Randwick one Saturday, which was owned by Callaghan. 'Jockey Johnny Hay said Paris Kiss should win, but that he thought stablemate Kiss of Gold was a certainty in the last.'

Paris Kiss scrambled in to win by a long neck at 3/1 and the owners cashed in. 'Ronnie Callaghan had $12,000 on it, and he put about $7,000 inside my top pocket. I went to the bathroom and split the money up, hiding a couple of thousand in every pocket of my suit.'

'Ronnie could drink a bit, and during our celebrations he pulled out $2000 from my top pocket and told (Randwick clocker) Mick O'Brien to go and throw it on Kiss of Gold for me. I didn't want to back it, and at 12/1 I would have had it each way anyway, but Ronnie said to have it straight out. It will win!'

In a tight finish, Kiss of Gold's jockey Noel Smith lost his whip and was beaten in a photo by one of Theo Green's horses. 'I'll never forget it. We still went out and celebrated, though. Ronnie thought it was funny, but I'm just so glad he didn't pull out the whole seven grand.'

Nothing typifies the ups and downs of the racing game than the story of Pat's star three-year-old Whisky Boy in the autumn of 1981. A $5000 purchase at the Newmarket Inglis sales, Pat so liked the son of Whiskey Road he brought a bunch of mates together along with wife Chrissy into the ownership.

When Whiskey Boy won at Canterbury in April, it earned enough prizemoney for a shot at the AJC Derby (2400m). A third in the Tulloch Stakes primed the gelding for the Group 1 classic – 'Every trainer's dream', Pat says, 'a Derby runner'. He had no doubt that this was the best horse he had trained since talking out a licence three years before.

'That horse had five gears,' Pat remarked at the time, adding, 'I didn't sleep for the whole week leading up to the Derby, I was so excited', revealing a trait that would follow him through every good horse he ever had.

Ridden by Denis McClune, Whiskey Boy was 'jogging' at the 600m when he was badly galloped on, snapping the bone in his near foreleg. As the Colin Hayes-trained Our Paddy Boy was being hailed the winner, Whiskey Boy was being pulled up at the back of the field and later had to be humanely put down.

'We all shed some tears after that loss', Pat says. A dream destroyed, he was possibly the best horse ever to wear Pat's orange and black colours.

The day after that fateful AJC Derby, Pat was feeling sorry for himself and attended the Easter Sales at Newmarket to have a few beers with close mates. When another of Whiskey Road's progeny entered the parade ring, he couldn't help himself – he liked the colt out of the mare Dalak, and even asked Melbourne trainers George Hanlon and Tommy Hughes Jnr for a second opinion. The colt, which raced as Attained, was knocked down to the Webster stable for $22,000. The horse raced in the same ownership as Whiskey Boy and won a couple of races for Pat, but had a bad habit of hanging in his races and was later sent to Melbourne.

After the Whisky Boy tragedy, there were lean times for the Webster stable. The stable would always be a small – albeit at racing's headquarters – but Pat, a hands-on trainer without a star horse in the stable, struggled to attract new owners with well-bred horses. 'I never was the top bidder at the sales, and most of the horses I got were cast-offs or home-bred', Pat says.

'Spider' Barker, the father of ill-fated jockey Noel Barker, was the stable foreman for Tommy Smith at the time. Barker would walk the great Kingston Town past Pat's stables on the way back to Tulloch Lodge after morning trackwork.

'I bet you wish you had one of these in your stables, Pat?' he would say light-heartedly when they walked past.

'Kingstown Town? You bet I would', Pat would reply.

Other trainers had V8s in their stable, Pat would often say. 'I had to make do with VWs.'

CHAPTER 8

The Clive Comet Sting

Gerry Harvey is well known as the multi-millionaire owner of the Harvey Norman electrical store empire. Along with close mate John Singleton, he has poured millions of dollars in to the Australian racing industry. Harvey has hundreds of racehorses spread across fifty trainers in Australia and New Zealand, and owns almost 600 broodmares in both countries.

'There is no reason behind which horses go to which trainers', Gerry Harvey tells me as he studies a large spreadsheet detailing his racing interests from the other side of a large desk at the Harvey Norman head office in Sydney. 'I just put them out there. Pat might get my best and he might get my worst, or a lot in between.'

Just over twenty years ago, Harvey bought the Magic Millions yearling sales concept, where horses purchased at the sales are eligible to run in million-dollar events, when the sales turnover was $23 million but the concept was effectively in administration. With partners John Singleton and Rob Ferguson, Harvey turned the Magic Millions into the premier sales event in the country, taking the mantle from William Inglis & Sons and New Zealand Bloodstock. After buying his partners out some years ago, today the Magic Millions turns over $370 million a year.

'If you had told anyone in the industry twenty years ago that Magic Millions would knock off Inglis, they would have thought you to be crazy. Inglis devotes 100 per cent of their time to their business, where I can only give a small percentage of my time to the Magic Millions. Inglis has two big sales mastheads in Sydney and Melbourne, where we have the four others in Queensland, Adelaide, Perth and Hobart.'

In the early 1970s, Harvey pioneered a stallion and racing syndication that would help shape Pat Webster's career as a trainer. 'Gerry Harvey has been my main client for almost forty years now', Pat says. 'He and wife Katie Page have been exceedingly loyal to me over the years. Gerry and his good mate Singo had horses with Theo Green, who recommended me to them.'

'I was slightly ahead of the game, as I was in many aspects of my business life, and was able to see the value in stallion syndications before anyone else', Harvey says. 'Racing syndications were around in the 1970s, but I was the first to syndicate a good horse to stand at stud.' Gypsy Kingdom, a son of Planet Kingdom, was that horse.

'Today, champion horses are purchased and syndicated as stallions all around the world', he says. 'John Singleton and I did the same thing with AJC Spring Champion Stakes winner Best Western in 1981. When Best Western was syndicated, the horse was valued at $6 million, which was an Australian record.'

An advertisement from the period in one of Pat's many scrapbooks is of Gerry Harvey offering punters a 'money back guarantee' if the selected Best Western progeny failed to win a race. The trainers advertised were Brian Mayfield Smith and Kerry Walker at Rosehill, and Randwick's Pat Webster.

Pat was always looking to get ahead in a tough game but, like every stable, he had his share of bad luck. Fearless Raider, a winner of the Christmas Cup at Hawkesbury, became cast in his box and went berserk, fatally injuring himself and bleeding out. Another, named Lawson, was killed when a wooden fence paling speared through his chest during a track gallop. Schuss looked a good horse in the making, but an exasperated trainer told pressmen that that the nag needed more ground. 'About twenty acres or so!'

But Pat was tantalisingly close to success. In fact, he could touch it. In the autumn of 1983, Pat received a phone call from Queensland trainer Doug Bougoure who said he was bringing down a promising horse for the AJC Derby. Could Pat find a box for him at Randwick? The horse's name was Strawberry Road.

Strawberry Road's potential was untapped when he landed in Sydney and was stabled with Pat Webster's team. With regular jockey Bill Cullen unavailable, Bougoure asked Pat who should ride the colt first up in the Hobartville Stakes (1400m). 'I suggested Maurice Logue because I knew his father "Doc" Logue. Doc was good friends with Betty and Tiger in the bush and he also operated a gravel truck alongside my dad. So, I've known Maurice forever.'

Logue was an up and coming jockey in Sydney's ranks, who would sensationally lose the ride on Golden Slipper favourite Sir Dapper the following month to the more experienced Ron Quinton. 'I always felt for Maurice Logue. The same thing had happened to me as a jockey, being replaced on a good horse in a big race, but it's part of the game.'

At his first start in Sydney, Strawberry Road ran a good second to Golden Slipper winner Marscay in the Hobartville Stakes. Logue was replaced by Cullen in his next three starts before the colt won the Rosehill Guineas (2000m) with Mick Dittman on top. Maurice Logue later became head of Racing NSW Apprentice Jockey School and still maintains Strawberry Road was the best horse he ever rode.

In one of the most authoritative performances in the time-honoured classic, Strawberry Road won the 1983 AJC Derby by 12 lengths on a bog track, beating Veloso, trained by Pat's Randwick neighbour Mal Barnes. But Strawberry Road almost missed his date with racing history.

'Doug and the owners liked to have a drink at the Doncaster Hotel. The day after a big session I got a phone call at my stables from the handicapper informing me I had ten minutes to come down to the AJC offices and accept Strawberry Road for the Derby. They couldn't raise Doug anywhere.'

Pat paid the acceptance fee for the Derby out of his own pocket, and then thought the trainer might want to accept for the Sydney Cup (3200m) as well. Since the AJC Derby had been switched to autumn in 1979, three-year-olds had dominated the two-mile race, with Double Century (1979), Kingston Town (1980) and Our Paddy Boy (1981) winning in consecutive years.

'I wasn't sure, so I accepted for both races. But I had to look and see that I had enough money in my cheque account to cover it first. It not like today when the ATC send you an invoice to pay. You had to pay up front.'

After the Derby win, the Strawberry Road team celebrated at a swank restaurant in Woollahra, inviting Pat and wife Chrissy who also brought along their stable jockey Craig Hyeronimus. 'Halfway through the night, one of the owners piped up and said, "I don't know why you accepted for the Sydney Cup". He said, "We have no intention of running him in Sydney again".' The owners were going to return to Brisbane and target their hometown Derby with their new star.

'I told the owner that I was only doing what I thought was right, but he got "on the piss" and kept on bringing it up. I was never one to suffer fools so I told him, "Well, if you're still not happy with what I did you can take the horse out of my stables". And that's what they did'.

The owners placed Strawberry Road in Mal Barnes' stable next door to Pat. Ad-man John Singleton owned Veloso and would go one better when he bought into Strawberry Road at the end of his three-year-old season. Strawberry Road would win the Cox Plate later than year before racing successfully overseas, including an unlucky fifth in the 1984 Prix de l'Arc de Triomphe in France.

'For a time in 1983,' Pat reflects, 'the best two horses in Australia – Strawberry Road and Veloso – were stabled side by side each other at Randwick – next to me!'

There was another horse in close proximity to Pat that would grab racing headlines later that year. Trained by Pat's brothers-in-law Jim and Greg

Lee, Kiwi-bred gelding Hayai finished unplaced in Strawberry Road's AJC Derby but, in the spring of 1983, he won the AJC Metropolitan (2600m) and the VATC Caulfield Cup (2400m). The 'Metrop' was held at Warwick Farm that year because Randwick was undergoing renovations, but Hayai proved his class by then winning the Caulfield Cup on a wet track, and backing up to take the Tancred Stakes (2400m) at Rosehill and a second Metropolitan Handicap (run at Randwick) the following year.

'I remember sitting in the lounge room at our home in Clovelly Road yahooing because Hayai led all the way in the Caulfield Cup at 25/1', Pat says. 'Our land and water rates were overdue, and we had our last $25 on him which paid our bill. And I wasn't even a punter!'

The Lees got their 'good horse' early in their training careers and were able to build up their stable, renamed Hayai Lodge, on this early success. Conversely, brother-in-law Pat had to wait until the end for his career to get his champion. 'I was just happy to be mentioned in their press reports', Pat says. 'They'd tell the journos, "Our brother-in-law Pat Webster trains too …"'

At the start of 1984, Pat was in a car crash on his way to the track and suffered two fractured discs in his back. Then he was involved in a stable accident which reinjured his back and required surgery on his knee. These setbacks led him to reduce his stable from a high of sixteen horses to just ten, turning away several new additions in the process.

But Pat was working on a long-range sting that would end up changing his life overnight.

In 1980, hardy New Zealand gelding Clive Comet won the Ipswich Cup when trained by AR 'Nobby' Gregory. A stayer of some ability, the horse raced more than 100 times during his career for a modest eight wins. Clive Comet returned to Australia as a nine-year-old in the spring of 1983, without much success – it must be said – but there was something about the hardy gelding that Pat Webster liked. He believed that the horse had one good win left in him, and perhaps a betting plunge could be pulled off.

With 'Nobby' Gregory returning to New Zealand, Pat came to an agreement with the old trainer for Clive Comet to remain in Australia under Pat's guidance, and to go halves in the nomination fees and prizemoney won. In the summer of 1983-84, the gelding ran a series of unlucky fourths in three 2400m races in top company – the Christmas Cup at Rosehill, the Summer Cup and Tattersall's Cup at Randwick – before Pat got a handle on what the horse needed.

'I couldn't afford to turn the horse out for too long, but he was walking around the stable like an old trotter and needed a short spell. At the time, we had some friends who had built GT Spelling Park at North Gosford – Allen and Julie Putland. I told my jockey Craig Hyeronimus that we'll give the horse an oil-based steroid and send him up to the spelling paddocks for a month and then bring him back on a good feed regime and see what happens'.

Oil-based steroids were entirely legal at the time, and most geldings were given them so that they could stand up to the rigors of hard training. Incredibly, given Clive Comet had raced for so long over so many seasons, he had never been given a course of steroids.

'We gave Clive Comet a steroid and he came up great, so we gave him one every fortnight after that. He was rising ten so he really needed it. We also put him on a corn diet and the horse was jumping over the moon. He was roaring.'

Pat has never been a hard worker of his horses, so when Clive Comet came back into his stable after a short spell, he had Craig Hyeronimus work the gelding at even pace over 1000m. 'Craig said, "Boss, this horse is flying. I can't hold him. Find a race for him at Randwick and he'll win first up."'

Pat picked out a 1400m Welter Handicap on Easter Saturday, 1984, at the height of the Randwick Autumn Carnival. 'I led him around the stable and put bandages on him so people would think he wasn't going that good', Pat says. He didn't trial the horse, just worked him in the dark when no-one was looking.

Mick O'Brien was a clocker at Randwick, and a stable punter, so Pat brought him into the sting because, as Pat says, 'Mick never missed a bloody thing at the track'. On the Tuesday before the designated race, Clive Comet needed a good hit-out on the course proper over 1000m but Pat didn't want to show his hand. Mick O'Brien reported in the newspaper that the horse that worked the best time of the morning was Clive Comet's stablemate, Steel a Babe.

'Steel A Babe was black, and Clive Comet looked black in the dark', Pat laughs. 'It was an "easy" mistake to make.'

Pat conscripted stable punter Trevor Stuckey and bookmaker Dick Greene on the planned betting plunge. Everything had to be timed to perfection. Clive Comet opened up at 33/1 but blew out to more than double that price before bookies were hit with a series of bets. Pat told his jockey to let the field go early and not to panic.

'Craig rode the horse perfectly', Pat says. 'He was back second last smoking his pipe and I was thinking, "Go now, son, go now" but he had them all covered.'

Hyeronimus brought Clive Comet home with a withering run to beat Holborn Court, ridden by Ron Quinton, by a half-length with 3/1 favourite Uno Petero running third. Although the horse paid $24.45 on the tote, or about 50/1 for a 50-cent unit, the gelding officially started at 80-1 around the country. SP bookies lost so much money that some couldn't pay out.

'Punters did not share the joy of Clive Comet's connections when the nine-year-old gelding, starting at 80-1, came from last to win the Vaucluse Handicap (1400m) at Randwick yesterday', journalist Ian Manning reported in the *Sunday Herald* the following day. 'But trainer Pat Webster, who had set Clive Comet for the event, sported a large smile as he pranced into the enclosure to greet the aged horse and his apprentice rider, Craig Hyeronimus.'

'Don't worry about the price, we've had our money on', Webster told the press. 'I though he was a good thing and couldn't believe the odds. Fancy getting 80/1 on a good thing! A nine-year-old gelding is hardly the type of horse to back with any confidence but I reckon he thinks he is only two …. (and) who am I to make him think any different?'

Stable backers had an estimated $10,000 each way on Clive Comet, although Pat's wager was slightly more modest.

'We didn't have mobile phones back then, but there was a little blue pickup phone on one of the walls of our stables. The phone rang the next morning and it was Trevor Stuckey. "Dick and me had a meeting last night and this is how much we had on Clive Comet for you. Is that enough?"

'Was it enough? Of course it was! That Sunday night, I met them at the Chinese restaurant at Cronulla Leagues Club and they organised a cake with sparklers on it with Clive Comet written all over it.' Stuckey and Green gave Pat a large wad of money wrapped in newspaper which he took straight home.

Pat had never seen so much money in his life. 'Some years earlier, a bookmaker named Lloyd Tidmarsh had been robbed of the day's winnings and murdered in his own home, so I was frightened having that much money in the house over the Easter long weekend', Pat admits. 'I put the money inside the bag of an old vacuum cleaner for safe keeping and took it around to a bloke called Bobby Reid who owned the Duke of Gloucester Hotel. I walked in with the vacuum cleaner under my arm and he said, "Thanks mate, but I don't need any rooms cleaned".'

Pat explained his predicament. The publican put the money in his safe.

Pat is coy about how much money he won on the Clive Comet sting, but it was enough for him and Chrissy to sell their home in Clovelly Road and buy a larger house in Eastern Avenue, Kensington.

'I had been at the track some weeks before and Theo Green told me that he was looking at a house in Eastern Avenue for his star apprentice Darren Beadman to buy. It was going to auction through Raine & Horne and I found out the name of the guy who owned it. It was a beautiful house, but

I didn't want to wait for the auction. I couldn't sleep so I went around to the home and knocked on the door.'

The local dentist who owned the property had emptied the house ahead of the auction and the only furniture inside was a bed and a grand piano. 'I asked him how much he wanted for the house. When he told me, I asked if he would throw in the grand piano. He said for an extra $500 I could have that too.'

Pat went around to see the local real estate agent in charge of the auction. 'He told me he couldn't sell it before the auction so I asked him if an extra $500 would change his mind. He rang the owners and said to me, if you pay an extra $500 you can have the house. We signed the papers the next day.'

Pat and Chrissy got the home they always wanted, and the grand piano too.

A couple of days later Pat was at the track and was standing next to Theo Green when the veteran trainer remarked, 'You won't believe it, Pat, but that fucking house I was looking at for Darren, some bastard's bought it'.

'Theo didn't smoke or drink but he sure could swear', Pat laughs. 'I didn't have the heart to tell him it was me because I loved the guy and didn't want to upset him.'

'Oh well, Darren'll find something else', Green said. Months later, the veteran trainer was walking along Eastern Avenue with his wife Nona when he spotted Pat out the front of the home watering the garden.

'*You* bought the house!' Theo exclaimed. 'Good for you.'

CHAPTER 9

All At Sea

Jim Lee was working his horses at Randwick one morning in the mid-1980s when he called out to Pat Webster. 'Did you hear what happened to George? He's been found murdered.'

'What?'

Pat knew who the 'George' was that Jim was talking about straight away. George Brown was a fellow trainer, and a good friend to Pat and Chrissy Webster as well as their neighbour in Kensington. He also had a sturdy horse in his stable, a gelding named McGlinchey, which was getting good press for the struggling trainer. Pat and his wife had George over at their house for dinner and enjoyed the company of the quiet, slow talking divorcée.

'Murdered?'

On the night of April 2, 1984, the body of George Brown was found in a burnt-out Falcon on top of Bulli Pass, south of Sydney. The Wollongong coroner later ruled that Brown had been force-fed a large amount of alcohol by his killers, his arms and legs broken and his skull crushed by several blows to the head. Interestingly, but unsurprisingly, his wristwatch had stopped working at 10.56 pm, the time the car had been set alight with Brown's body inside it.

With the murder remaining unsolved for the past thirty-five years – NSW Police recently announced a $1 million reward for information leading to the arrest of those responsible – the rumour mill in racing circles has worked overtime. Brown's death was cast in a new light the following August following the 'Fine Cotton Ring-in' race at Eagle Farm in Brisbane. Disgraced trainer Hayden Haitana later told a journalist that he went through with the substitution of the gelding Fine Cotton with the better performing Bold Personality because a standover man had asked him, 'Do you want to end up like the trainer Brown?'

Had George Brown been murdered over another 'ring-in' that somehow went wrong? Two days before his death, Brown's horse Risley was well backed at Doomben but failed to run a place. Did he owe the wrong people a lot of money; or was a woman involved, his death the result of immense jealousy in a relationship gone wrong?

'I knew George better than others, but not that well that I knew what happened to him', Pat says. 'I told him we liked to have a beer at the Duke of Gloucester and did he want to come along? It might have even cost me a horse or two because people went into syndicates with him but it didn't matter. He was a champion bloke.'

But Pat doubts his friend was involved in any skulduggery. 'George was too nice a guy, and he wasn't a "player"', he says. He was just another battling trainer, someone described in press reports at the time as 'a moderate punter, doing it tough'.

Pat inherited some of the lesser horses from Brown's stable, including the aforementioned Steal A Babe, as well as some of his staff, hoping to do right by his racing mate.

Perhaps his murder will be solved one day, and the scales of justice will be set right for George Brown. 'I certainly hope so', says Pat.

***

Pat Webster loved Theo Green. Perhaps it was Pat's bush sensibility that appealed to the veteran Sydney trainer and noted mentor of apprentice jockeys. Maybe it was the fact that they had both worked on the wharfs before they became struggling trainers, but Pat says it was more likely because that he was a good listener and was always keen to learn from the best.

'And when Theo Green said something, you'd be a fool not to listen.'

Pat learned many important lessons from 'The Boss', as Green was known. 'Theo had a high-profile owner pull up at his stables one day in his big car who said, "I'm sorry Boss, I have some bad news. I need to take my horse out of your stables".

'Theo said, "Bad news? That's not bad news, son. I thought something was wrong with one of your family … of course, you can take your horse. You're a good payer; just go and pick up the papers from the office".'

The lesson was, if owners wanted to take their horses from you, let them go. There's no point training for unhappy owners.

Pat and Theo also shared another, more tragic bond. 'Theo Green had an apprentice named David Green (no relation) who often rode a horse called Misty Eyes for me. I rang Theo to book David for my horse one week and he explained he had just taken another ride in the same race. That's how Theo operated in booking rides for all his apprentices … first in, best-dressed.'

On March 8 1980, David Green was tragically killed when his mount, Bold Rachel, fell in the race at Rosehill. 'Theo never got over the death of young David Green. Racing had been so good to him and then that happened.'

The tragedy had a big impact on Pat too. 'That really affected me in a lot of ways. David Green was a beautiful person. If I'd called five minutes earlier, he might be alive today.'

Some trainers achieve the recognition of their peers with champion horses.

Theo Green achieved it through his development of champion jockeys. Green guided Gordon Spinks, Ron Quinton, John Duggan, Malcolm Johnston and Darren Beadman to the very top of their profession, but more importantly, he made them better people.

As eight-time premiership-winning jockey Ron Quinton once remarked, 'Every day with Theo, we were getting a lesson in life'. Inducted into the Australian Racing Hall of Fame in 2002, Green was lauded for teaching his charges 'about life, discipline and the invaluable attributes of loyalty and integrity'.

Green did more than just get jockeys ready for the racing game. He took kids off the streets and educated them in the toughest school there is ... if they wanted to learn. Although not all of them could make it to the top, they all benefitted from Green's tutelage.

Green had a remarkable life in racing. Weight problems ended his time as a jockey during the war years, but after stints as a miner, labourer and wharfie, he made enough money out of a promising boxing career to buy his first stables at Rosehill. Green trained there for many years before shifting to Randwick in 1971.

Theo Green enjoyed great success with horses such as Red Nose (third in the 1979 Melbourne Cup), champion filly Shaybisc and hardy Cups horse Starzam. In the mid-1980s, his two-year-olds Street Café and Inspired won the Blue Diamond Stakes and Golden Slipper respectively, while chestnut gelding At Sea emerged as one of the best sprinters of his generation. The son of Aurealis won three successive Carrington Stakes (1000m) between 1985 and 1987, before finishing a half-head second to Snippets in the same race in January 1988.

'At Sea could have been one of the great sprinters of all time', says John Singleton, 'but his elderly owner didn't want to fly to Melbourne to watch it race. He'd rather stay in Sydney and watch his horse win handicaps carrying 63kg and the like'.

In 1988, Green suddenly announced to the Sydney media that he planned to disperse his stable at the end of the racing year. His beloved wife Nona had contacted Parkinson's Disease and he was retiring immediately to care for her. When asked by his owners, including breeder Stuart Nivison (the owner of At Sea), who should take over the training of their horses, Green had no hesitation in nominating Pat Webster.

'Theo told me he was going to retire. He said, "I spoke to Mr Nivison, and you're getting At Sea".' All Pat could say was thanks. 'Things like that just weren't supposed to happen to a bloke like me.'

It was a great compliment from Green, not only to Pat's ability as a horseman but also his personality in dealing with high profile owners. Following Nivison's lead, bloodstock agent Philippa Duncan and New Zealand businessman Don Dick transferred their horses to Pat as well. For the first time in ten years, quality horses came Pat's way ... eight new horses in all – including Rainbow High, the promising Mariinksy and the well-bred three-year-old filly Bolshoi, a $500,000 purchase.

But the star addition to Pat's stable was the champion sprinter At Sea, the winner of sixteen races from his twenty-seven starts. Pat felt that this was his best chance to finally make his mark in Sydney's training ranks, before conceding that he didn't take over At Sea purely for the horse. He did it out of respect for Theo Green.

'That was the greatest compliment I ever received,' he said at the time, 'Theo having the faith in me as a trainer to do justice to a champion like At Sea'.

Already the winner of three editions of the Carrington Stakes, an Apollo Stakes (1400m), Expressway Stakes (1200m), Canterbury Stakes (1300m) and five other listed races, At Sea was a rising eight-year-old when Webster took over as trainer. As he colourfully described at the time, he was on 'a shellacking to nothing'.

'If the horse wins, it's the horse; but if he loses it's the trainer's fault', Pat observed.

Complicating matters further was the recent decision by racing authorities to ban steroids, which had been used for decades to assist geldings to stand up to the rigors of racing. Like a lot of trainers at the time, Pat was a vocal supporter of steroids – he believed At Sea needed them to compete at the highest level now that he was an aged gelding – although he would change his stance later. 'It was ultimately the right decision to ban them', he says today.

'At Sea had been getting a steroid every fortnight since he was two years old. Without steroids for the first time in his racing career, At Sea developed splits on both legs and his back molars fell out. When he was eating corn, it would fall out the sides of his mouth. The horse developed massive corns on his feet because it was going through withdrawals, so it was quite a battle to train him.'

Pat was unsure if At Sea's legs would stand up to the preparation so he mixed his light trackwork with trips to the beach at Botany Bay. 'We couldn't gallop him hard. We had to "cuddle him" to give him a chance to recuperate from trackwork.'

And the old chestnut had other quirks too. 'You cannot be out by a minute with his routine, otherwise he'll get restless', Pat commented at the time. 'You have to be precise with his movements otherwise he will jack up.' It helped enormously that At Sea's regular attendant, Greg Baxter, arrived each morning and afternoon to look after the horse, while trackwork rider Paul Williams had a great affinity with the horse.

At Sea was a difficult horse to train because he was such a puller in his work. To offset this, At Sea wore a special noseband in his trackwork. When he pulled excessively, the noseband cut his wind off momentarily which caused the horse to ease off on the pulling so he could catch his breath.

It was a worrying time getting the horse ready for a fifth consecutive start in the Carrington Stakes in January 1989. 'Everything was going fine until the rain came,' he confided in journo Rod Gallegos, 'and everyone knows he is a duffer on tracks that are anything more than dead'.

Pat had another in the long stretch of sleepless nights leading up to a big race before waiting until the last minute to declare At Sea a definite starter at Randwick. With champion jockey Darren Beadman on top, it was time to deliver.

In the Carrington, At Sea loomed up to win at 200m, and for a few strides it looked like he was going to go on with it, but in-form mare Sunalong Lass kicked clear to win by two lengths from the fast finishing Paris Weekend. At Sea ran a creditable third, carrying a topweight of 60kg, with the winner running a race record of 57 seconds flat.

At his next start, At Sea finished fourth in the Challenge Stakes (1000m) behind the three-year-old Groucho. In a race full of hard luck stories, At Sea was less than a length from the winner and ran a faster time than in winning the race the previous year. If Pat was disappointed, he didn't show it. 'Darren was at him all the way and he never had a chance to get balanced', the trainer told journalist Max Presnell. 'I'm not making excuses but [At Sea] will be better over 1200m.'

In the Expressway Stakes (1200m) the following month, Ron Quinton deputised for the suspended Darren Beadman on At Sea and got to within a neck of the winner, Groucho. 'He ran a great race, as you expect, but he just seems to have lost some of his zip', Quinton told Pat after the race. 'When the other one [Groucho] went, he couldn't accelerate like he used to.' Showing the depth of the race, champion sprinter Campaign King was a close third as the 10/9 favourite.

At Sea finally gave Pat his first group win when he won the Group 2 Canterbury Stakes (1200m) in March 1989. The gelding had won the same race the previous year, and Pat knew he would be judged harshly if the horse could not salute at his fourth start for the stable. In a driving finish, regular jockey Darren Beadman took At Sea to the front and held off the fast finishing Campaign King, with third Groucho.

'At Sea was an aristocrat you couldn't help but respect', Pat remarked. 'It was such a relief when he won. What a horse!'

Following At Sea's win, Pat sought the solitude of the public area, away from everyone. Sipping on a can of Toohey's New he remembers shedding a tear or two 'for myself and for the horse'. For the next twenty minutes, he reflected on the pressure he put on himself in proving he was the right trainer for such a good horse.

'It was the biggest thrill I'd had in racing at the time, and my biggest thrill up until Happy Clapper gave me my first Group I win', he says.

And never again would he doubt his own ability as a trainer.

But the winter of 1989 was a wet one and Pat knew it was pointless keeping At Sea in training so he sent the gelding for a well-earned spell. At Sea raced only two more times, finishing his career with an unplaced run in the 1990 Challenge Stakes, his sixth straight running in the race.

Pat had never had a horse good enough to name his stables after but after training At Sea he decided to name his Doncaster Avenue stables after the gelding. 'In my mind he was always Theo's horse', Pat explained at the time. 'People will call me a "mug liar" naming my stables after At Sea. (But) my thinking is it could be the last opportunity for At Sea to get the permanent recognition he deserves.'

Pat would often run into Theo Green in the ensuing years, pushing his wife Nona in a wheelchair down Eastern Avenue as the Parkinson's Disease gradually took hold of her body. Nona died in January 1999 and her devoted husband Theo collapsed at the official spreading of her ashes. Green passed away the following month, age seventy-four.

'Theo Green was a huge influence on me,' Pat says, 'and a great bloke who gave wonderful advice on life. Even now I often think to myself, what would Theo do in these circumstances?'

At Sea was the best horse Theo Green had trained in his long career, and Pat never thought he would ever find another one as good.

CHAPTER 10

Patrick's Story

As a teenager, Patrick Webster Jnr bailed up family friend, journalist Glenn Robbins, at Randwick races. 'Can you have a word with Dad?' Patrick asked. 'He doesn't want me to have anything to do with the racing game.'

Robbins was so moved by the boy's determination he wrote about it in his weekly column. 'Dad feels I have to have a trade', Patrick told the racing scribe. 'He feels it would mean something to me if I set myself goals and worked to achieve them.'

Patrick Jnr dreamed of being a jockey and trainer like his father and uncles. This was a kid who slept with a *Turf Monthly* magazine under his bed, got a stable pony for Christmas and hoped against hope that he wouldn't grow too tall to be a jockey.

'He would have loved to be a jockey', father Pat says. 'At home, he used to sit on a pillow at the end of the bed and flog the shit out of it with a whip while broadcasting the race. He was just so desperate.'

'Unfortunately, Pat and Patrick were the tallest boys in the Webster family for four generations', mother Chrissy adds. By the age of sixteen, Patrick's dream was over. 'Even when he was a boy, he'd say, "Don't buy my shoes so big mum". Forget it, I told him – you're going to be a big boy.'

Chrissy says that of her three children, it was Patrick who most loved everything about the sport – the breeding, the horses, the trainers, the jockeys, the big races and even the winning colours. 'He has a phenomenal memory', Chrissy adds, admitting that Patrick's life may have turned out very differently if he had become a jockey.

'Maybe.'

When Patrick was still at school, he loved to spend time with his father at the stables. Pat admits that he might have pushed Patrick away from that life because he wanted his son to have a trade … to do better than he did. Looking back now, Pat realises perhaps that's where Patrick was happiest – talking to his father about horses when he was organising the feeds after trackwork.

'We had some beautiful times there together', Pat says. 'I didn't care if my kids got into the game after they got a trade but it was a tough life, racing.'

'Dad was very strict growing up and didn't want us hanging around the stable', daughter Diane recalls. After sitting her HSC, Diane completed a diploma in real estate before stumbling into the recruitment business. Younger brother Wayne was a qualified chef before he joined his father in a training partnership in 2008. After leaving school Patrick began a six-year plumbing apprenticeship, which he finished, but the eldest son in the Webster family was also on another long, personal journey that would span the best part of twenty years …

Drug addiction.

It started off a series of minor things at first, Chrissy Webster says. Small items would go missing from the Webster home; then money disappeared, and then Patrick himself went missing. The situation quickly spiralled out of control and Patrick became a full-blown heroin addict, living on the streets and spending long periods in gaol before finally bringing his life under control.

Pat and Chrissy confronted their son about his addictions, searched for him when he went on benders and supported him in his rehabilitation. 'Finding him OD'd on the bathroom floor was hard', Pat says. 'Watching a paramedic drive a needle into our son's chest to bring him back to life was hard. But the doctor telling us that the "next four hours would determine if he lives or not" was the hardest.'

Patrick Webster Jnr was born in 1972, the first grandchild on Chrissy's side of the family and, being a male, a position of some importance.

'Was Patrick spoilt?' Chrissy asks herself. 'Probably. But we were young parents ourselves and we underestimated just how intelligent – and sensitive – Patrick was.'

When trainer Cec Rowles won the 1964 Golden Slipper with Eskimo Prince, high-profile owner Perc Galea brought a rocking horse for Cec's daughter. 'Greg and Jimmy Lee had been apprenticed to Cec,' Pat says, 'and when Patrick came along, Cec gave the rocking horse to him. He couldn't wait to get on it.'

Patrick was always competitive as a boy – a natural all-rounder, he made the 'rep' teams in football and cricket but when the pressure was on, his parents noticed, he struggled to deliver. 'It first registered with me when he was about nine or ten years old', Chrissy says. 'I said to Pat one night that I think we have a little problem with Patrick.'

That morning, Patrick had informed his mother that he had a stomachache and wouldn't be able to go to school. 'He was the captain of the red team at the sports carnival that day, but for some unknown reason he said he was sick so I took it at face value and kept him home.' When Chrissy went to pick Diane up from school, the boy asked immediately, 'Which team won?'

His team had won; only he wasn't there to take part in it.

Patrick was the most academically gifted of the Webster children – and artistic – but his grades suffered in high school. Enrolled in one of the better schools in the Eastern Suburbs, he started hanging around with new friends, mixing with the wrong crowd, and his behaviour changed.

'We could notice little things, or so we thought', Chrissy says. 'Patrick wasn't coming home on time and then we discovered he was drinking and smoking pot as a young teenager.' To make matters worse, the pot was laced with heroin, which was rare in those days, but making a real impact on the Eastern Suburbs in the late 1980s.

Like many teenagers, Patrick was threatened with boarding school by his worried parents if he didn't start towing the line. A casual teacher assaulted him in class one day, ripping the boy's shirt, and Chrissy's mother was so enraged she went up to the school and complained to the principal. Boarding school looked like the right option, although Patrick didn't want to leave his family, or the stables where he spent his spare time working with the jockeys and his favourite horses.

'We thought we were on top of the problem early,' Chrissy says, 'but when we couldn't isolate the problem, we thought we'd isolate Patrick from the problem.' His parents sent him to boarding school in Bowral.

'It wasn't an easy decision to send Patrick to boarding school – it expensive for a start', Pat says. 'We discussed it for a long time, so it wasn't an overnight decision.'

Patrick again rebelled. 'We thought he was just being disruptive,' Pats says, 'but we found out in a subsequent court case there was a very good reason why he didn't want to be there.' Back home for the holidays, he disappeared on the night before he was to return to school.

'I found him in the loft of my stables with the jockeys Matty Privato, Joey Galea and Shane Arnold', Pat says. 'That's where he was happiest.'

Patrick stayed at boarding school for a little over two years, but walked out just before his HSC exams. 'Patrick didn't say why he left school at the time, only that he didn't want to be there anymore', Chrissy says. His dorm master kept in touch with him, and Pat and Chrissy intimate that there may have been other issues there too, but the end result was Patrick's time at school had come to an abrupt end.

One of Pat's owners worked for Randwick Plumbing, so Pat asked his son if he wanted to be a plumber. Patrick completed his full trade, working in his spare time at Pat's stables, which at least offered him some stability. But soon he fell back in with some of his former schoolmates and old habits resurfaced.

'Patrick and his mate Mick were hanging around a unit in Randwick, sourcing drugs', Pat remembers. 'I knocked on the door and they were inside, high as kites.' Pat got the boys outside and they admitted to him that they had taken heroin. 'I took them both to Prince Alfred Hospital, which had a drug outreach program. Mick went in and stayed in; Patrick went in one door and out another on the other side of the hospital.'

Patrick finished up a heroin addict while Mick, who is still a good mate, never touched drugs again. It was literally a revolving door moment in their lives.

'Friends would tell us that they saw him living on the street', Chrissy says. 'That was terribly hard to hear as a parent. We took him to Mudgee to get away from the city and he thought it was snowing he was so cold. We talked him through the whole detox.'

But it didn't last.

'I put bars on the windows of our house at Eastern Avenue and put a deadlock on the doors in a bid to make him go "cold turkey" as they say', says Pat. 'That was hard too. But the really hard part is lying in bed and hearing an ambulance siren late at night and thinking, *Is it our son?*'

Everyone tried to help Patrick, they admit. Although he invariably used it for drugs, Chrissy's brothers would give Patrick money because they loved him, and the same thing happened with a wide network of friends.

'They would rather Patrick have money than steal it from a stranger', Pat says.

Pat and Chrissy did everything they could, although they admit that they were totally unprepared to deal with what Patrick was going through. 'We went to counselling ourselves because we had no idea what went wrong', Chrissy recalls. 'A mother told her story about her drug-addicted son and I couldn't believe what I heard. They asked me if I had anything I wanted to say, but I couldn't speak. I realised then just how big a problem drugs were in the community. It took me a while to get my head around it, but I think Pat summed it up fairly quickly. "Buckle up, we're going on a ride here."'

'The Chinese have a name for heroin,' says Chrissy, 'the "Little White Lady". I remember saying to Pat, if she can replace the love of a parent, then we're in a lot of trouble.'

Pat and Chrissy felt for their other children too. 'But they were okay and Patrick wasn't,' Chrissy rationalises, 'so he was our primary focus. And they loved him too.' If either of the children complained about the amount of time and energy spent supporting Patrick, Chrissy would say in her down-to earth way, 'If this had been you, we would be doing the same thing, so thank God that it's not'.

The kids were always close, Chrissy says. 'They love each other and are very protective of each other.'

Pat and Chrissy also became a tighter parenting unit. 'We never asked, why us?' Chrissy says. 'At that time, Prime Minister Bob Hawke's daughter was also fighting addiction, so it could happen to any family. But you don't just learn to "handle it" – we had to be strong with each other and with Patrick. It sounds corny, but the answer is love, and our love for Patrick meant never wanting to give up on him.'

It was suggested that Patrick to go to the United States to get medical treatment but, because he had a criminal record, he couldn't get a visa. Instead, the Websters opted to take him to Israel to be treated at the famous Dr Waismann Heroin Clinic. 'The morning before we left for overseas, Patrick disappeared and Pat was driving over median stripes in the Eastern Suburbs looking for him', says Chrissy. 'He'd gone to buy some racing magazines to read on the plane.'

It was a long trip, and Chrissy and Patrick had to stay overnight in Jakarta, although they weren't allowed out of the airport. A doctor gave Patrick some Valium to take on the trip and he was kicking the seats in front of him because he was so irritated.

'By the time we got to Israel, he was pretty much detoxed', Chrissy says.

But once in Israel, Patrick connected with other drug addicts and was able to source heroin on the streets. 'The clinic knocked him out and put a chemical through his system to detox him and it worked in the short term. When Patrick walked back through the gates at Sydney International Airport, he looked beautiful.'

'Did it take? No.' she says.

'That's what I've learned about drug addicts. You're wasting your time trying to help an addict if they're not ready to get help. It's easy to say let them go to gaol, let them bottom out, but you can't because you love them so much. Patrick didn't want to quit drugs back then. He was still running with the devil and no-one could have reached him.'

Not so strangely, when Patrick was a child and he had to get an injection, he was absolutely petrified of needles, Pat says. 'I remember coming home from the doctors and saying to Chrissy, "Well that's one thing we don't have to worry about".'

'I had to take him to my sister-in-law's surgery, who is a doctor', Chrissy says. 'Patrick had … damaged his veins through the overuse of needles. She said to him, "You're clean now but I know you still have drugs on your mind. If you ever use that vein again you will drop down dead. End of story". I thought that if Patrick could comprehend that, we had a chance of winning the battle.'

But when it came to their son's addiction, the Websters were realists. 'We're going to have him as a drug addict or not at all', Pat says. 'I said to Chrissy, "What's it going to be then? We have to keep soldiering on". And that's what we chose to do.'

In between stints in prison, Patrick moved home to live with his parents at Eastern Avenue. It was a case of one step forward, two steps back. 'Chrissy was lying in bed early one morning when she sat bolt upright. "I can't breathe, somethings wrong", she said.'

Pat and Chrissy went upstairs to where Patrick was living and they could hear the water running in the shower. 'We were calling out to him to open the door but there was no answer. We couldn't open the door so Chrissy crawled through a side window into the bathroom. That's when the doctor said the next four hours would tell us whether he'll live or not.'

'When we almost lost him, I said that's just a taste of what it would feel like to lose him for good and it will stay with us until the day we die', Chrissy says. They would never give up on him.

'And really, that's what makes me want to help others', says Pat, alluding to his current role with Racing NSW counselling young jockeys. 'You have to give back. We can't help everyone, because some people don't want to be helped, but I rely on Chrissy a lot because she's been through it with Patrick and she has really good protective instincts.'

'We always help people who ask', says Chrissy. 'That's just who we are.'

Chrissy Webster knows the difference between a prescription drug user, an ice addict, a heroin addict, and a dope smoker. When someone close to the stable developed a cocaine addiction, Chrissy knew straight away. 'I could tell because I've seen it all with Patrick.'

The Websters take comfort in the fact that Patrick has never been gaoled for selling drugs, but it's a very small comfort. 'His last stint was three years,' Pat says, 'but he finally got off heroin and has been clean ever since'.

Pat and Chrissy also made the difficult decision not to visit their son in prison the last time he was gaoled. They wrote to him, of course, and spoke to him on the phone, but the main reason they didn't visit him was because they were protecting Patrick's teenage son, Jack. Pat and Chrissy Webster have raised the boy from infancy and, as their daughter Diane says, 'something good came out of all that chaos'.

'In the early days I went almost every weekend to visit Patrick in gaol,' says sister Diane, 'spending two hours on Saturday with him. After I moved to Melbourne to live, I would schedule at least two business trips a year in NSW so I could go and visit him'. It also made her less judgmental as a person.

'When you see an addict on the street,' Diane says, 'you don't know the story or circumstances about how they got there so don't judge. I also understand when people get to their breaking point dealing with drug addiction because we were almost there as a family. But for me, Patrick's more successful than any of us because he's beaten his addiction. It's like climbing Everest – we're so proud of him'.

No doubt, Patrick has heeded his mother's stark advice to 'spend the rest of the time God gives you enjoying your life'. Everyone has good and bad days, she says, but her eldest son is in a good place now, both physically and mentally.

'It's the best he's been in twenty years,' she says. 'He's very disciplined in what he eats and how he trains because he wants to look his best, and in the end that was the motivation he needed to get off drugs.'

Today, Patrick lives in a beautiful guest house on the family property at Kulnura as he slowly rebuilds his life. The young man who greets me at the farm gate is both friendly and personable – superbly fit, he looks much younger than his forty-seven years – and is possessed of a sharp intelligence, especially when you start discussing horses.

Patrick Webster Jnr is finally his own man.

CHAPTER 11

Don't Die Wondering

In the early 1990s, Pat Webster was approached about standing for local council. The Resident's and Ratepayers Association asked him if he would stand as an alderman for the West Ward of Randwick City Council. Pat said yes.

'They were upset over the cutting down of a couple of trees in the area and wanted change', Pat says. 'Who knew I was a "closest greenie"?'

Pat had lived in the local area long enough to know of the goings on in the Randwick area. 'There was a lot of traffic coming through Eastern Avenue,' Pat says, 'and there were usual rumours of branch stacking and such shenanigans. It was just my way of trying to help'.

Announcing his candidacy, Pat handed out how to vote cards at Doncaster Shopping Centre, while fellow trainer Bill Mitchell handed out pamphlets in support of his election bid. 'I became fitter than some of my horses walking the streets of Randwick and Kensington handing out how to vote cards.'

All was set for polling day, until noted sports journalist and boxing promoter Bill Mordey rang Pat at home. 'What are you doing?' Bill asked down the line.

'I told him I was standing for the local council. "Some old lady will be ringing you at night complaining that there is dog shit on a median strip in Kensington", he told me bluntly.'

Pat thought about it for a moment and said, 'You're right. See you later'.

Pat's political career was over. Although he was still on the ballot, he preferenced all his votes to his running mate.

He would stick to training horses.

***

In February 1991, Chrissy Webster threw Pat a surprise 40th birthday party at Randwick's 'Newmarket' stables, owned by the William Inglis & Son livestock company. The historic precinct, later heritage listed, was also home to Bernie Byrnes' stables where Pat had undertaken his jockey apprenticeship in the 1960s.

'The Big Stable', as it was known, was built around 1880 behind the Newmarket Hotel, from which it took its name. Measuring approximately 40m x 17m, it had a timber frame construction with external walls of painted weatherboard and a corrugated iron roof. 'The core of the design is a large central space roofed at a high level with clerestory glazed sashes on both sides, for the full length of the building', the official heritage guide describes. 'Stabling boxes open from each side of this space. Above each row of stabling extends a wide gallery space with open balustrading between the posts of the main structure.'

Pat had taken Chrissy there only once, to attend the Inglis Easter sales one year, but the idea of hosting a surprise birthday party for him there intrigued her. 'My friend Robin Christie and I were looking for a project to work on, so we threw ourselves into planning our husband's 40th birthday parties. I remember looking at the old clock hanging in the centre of the Newmarket complex and thought, what a great place for a party!'

The biggest hurdle was convincing John Inglis and Bernie Byrnes to let Chrissy hold the party there. Trainer Byrnes would have to clear out his entire stables for the night so they could use the main area, so she knew it wasn't going to be easy.

'Mr Byrnes could be something of an old grump, but when I spoke to him, he said, "Well young lady, I give you ten points for even coming through the door to ask me something like that".' Byrnes agreed to help, on one condition. 'He didn't want Pat's father Spider on the premises. I never knew why, but they obviously had a huge falling out.'

It was then Chrissy made a decision she was later to regret, although she made it for all the right reasons. 'I decided this event would not be for family members – I would host another get together for the family at our place.' Only 100 people were invited, mainly friends and colleagues in the racing industry who had known Pat for at least half his life. That was Chrissy's criteria.

Chrissy employed the best caterers, hired a jazz band and stocked an ample supply of beer and wine. 'Tables were set out in a huge horseshoe and people had to dress in orange and black, Pat's stable colours.' No gifts were required, guests were instructed to just come along and have a good time.

Attended by many of Pat's fellow trainers, owners, jockeys and stable staff, Chrissy enticed Glenn Robbins to write a special edition of the *Newmarket News* for the occasion:

> **Randwick trainer Pat Webster has been summonsed before the Australian Jockey Club committee to 'show cause' why he should not be warned off all racecourses around the world ... Webster has to defend an alleged charge 'of failing to hit his kick when in a round of drinks in the Oaks Bar at Randwick races on Saturday'.**

Pat, of course, knew nothing about his wife's meticulous planning. 'She dressed me up in a tuxedo, blindfolded me and sent me off in a hire car. I didn't have a clue what was going on. Kenny Stone, Theo Green's foreman, has never forgiven me for not inviting him, but it had nothing at all to do with me.'

Pat says he made up for the gaffe by inviting Stone to the family party at his home and allowing him to sing with the band that night. 'And he can't sing a bloody note!'

Chrissy had a videographer film the birthday bash, including speeches from John Inglis, Bernie Byrnes and the man of the moment, husband Pat – with one minor glitch. 'The video guy had such a great night mixing with everyone, he forgot to turn the sound on.'

Pat was in a good place as the 1990s rolled round. The success of At Sea had given him the self-confidence to succeed, and the former bush jockey had worked hard to establish himself among his training peers at racing headquarters.

A newspaper article of the period notes that Pat was 'doing well with a small string' alongside fellow trainers Bill Mitchell, Brian Mayfield Smith, Anthony Cummings, Grahame Begg, Bobby Thomson, Les Bridge, Ron Quinton and Alan Bell. There was camaraderie among the new breed of trainers, but also fierce competition.

When Pat's filly Miss Worthington took flight behind the barriers and dumped jockey Darren Beadman before a big race at Randwick, she ran amok on the course proper and completed a full lap before the race could start. As the filly sailed down the straight – sans jockey, all on her lonesome – Anthony Cummings turned to his Randwick neighbour and said, 'Well that was a winning gallop, Pat'. Cummings then went out and won the race with his good filly Tristanagh.

Miss Worthington had done the same thing at trackwork the previous Thursday, yanking Pat's elbow so hard that he reinjured it while it was on the mend after a recent stable accident. As he watched all his hard work with the filly go down the gurgler in a couple of minutes of mayhem, Pat didn't know whether to laugh or cry. Or perhaps, do both.

Pat worked hard to cultivate good relationships with his fellow trainers. He classes Cummings, Gai Waterhouse, Ron Quinton and John O'Shea as close friends. 'Ron has been a close mate for close on fifty years', he says.

'Gai was the first to congratulate me after Happy Clapper's success. She was genuinely happy for us … a beautiful person.'

When Patrick Jnr was going through rehab, John O'Shea was one of the first to offer moral support. 'I took John to a rehab session at a chapter of the Salvation Army because he genuinely wanted to know and understand what we were going through as parents. The "happy clappers" were out in force that night, and John and I had to clap along as they sang their salvation songs. He was a bit reticent at first, I think.'

The irony of this 'happy clapper' experience is not the least bit lost on Pat, years before a gelding called Happy Clapper would change his life.

Pat and Chrissy were also very close to Brian Mayfield Smith when the Rosehill trainer toppled TJ Smith for the trainer's premiership in the 1986-87 season. 'Brian lived at our property at Mudgee for 12-18 months when he first retired. We got on really well, and if I was short a couple of horses in my stable, he'd give me a couple of pre-trainers. He was another hard task-master, just like TJ.'

The year he celebrated his 40th birthday, Pat was in trouble with racing officials when they fined him $8000 for a positive swab taken from a horse called Staggers. After the John Singleton-owned gelding ran fifth in a lowly maiden at Randwick on Melbourne Cup day, the horse tested positive for lignocaine. The drug had been in the news earlier that year when champion two-year-old Tierce returned a positive reading after winning the Golden Slipper. Tierce's trainer Clarrie Connors was fined $15,000 – $10,000 for the Slipper and $5000 for the AJC Sires – but connections were allowed to keep both races.

'Not only did stewards fine me $8000,' Pat says, 'but they disqualified the horse from the race, which meant we lost the fifth-place prizemoney. They didn't do that to Tierce!'

It was later discovered that one of Pat's stable hands had administered a non-prescription cream called xylocaine, involving just 2 per cent of the illegal drug, on a cut on a horse's mouth. No one in the stable had been informed of the application on the previous weekend. Although Pat knew that the drug could not have had an impact on the horse's performance, he supervised all administration of drugs and knew that he held ultimate responsibility for his stable.

Pat pled guilty to the charge of bringing a horse to the races having administered to it a prohibitive substance. The $8000 fine was later reduced on appeal. It was all part of the hustle and bustle of racing.

When the Webster stable won the last at Randwick soon after, the winner Sail to Success paid $69.90 on the tote for a 50c unit. With the owners having $1000 each way on the winner, and Pat a little less, the stable was well into their celebrations when stable foreman Terry Mercer joined them, still wearing his work gear. With the group in great cheer, Mercer pulled Pat to one side and whispered in his ear, 'Remember that stuff we give horses going out for a spell?'

'The stuff that is illegal if applied to a horse seven days before a race?' Pat asked.

'Well, I thought the horse was going out for a spell and I gave that to him this morning', Mercer told him.

Pat was already contemplating the headlines and mandatory six-month suspension when he quietly informed the others in the party that there was a problem.

Only then did Mercer tell Webster he was joking.

'Tony Hartnell from Racing NSW had a stud at Moruya on the NSW South Coast. Terry Mercer was his stud manager, and he later landed on my doorstep with his wife Kylie asking for a job.' Pat didn't like the idea of a husband and wife working together in a stable – it's far too hard on a marriage, he believes – but Terry became his stable foreman and Kylie worked for another trainer. Both lived at Pat's stables on Doncaster Avenue.

Years later, Terry Mercer returned to Moruya to work for a rival stud. 'A nicer, more knowledgeable person you couldn't meet. Then Tony Hartnell rang me one night and said, "Pat, Terry's shot himself". It didn't sink in at all, so I asked, "Is he all right?"'

'Pat, he's dead.'

Mercer, the joker of the Webster stable, had taken his own life on a lonely beach.

'The racing life has always been hard, even during the good times', Pat says. 'Physically hard, mentally hard and financially hard.'

Pat and Chrissy Webster have always been motivated to 'have a go', to make something of their lives for them and for their children. 'When the kids were still at school, we won a trip to for two to Fiji at a school disco. There's no way we could have afforded to go as a family without winning that trip, but we decided to upgrade and change the destination to Hawaii so the whole family could go.'

It was probably the first family holiday the Websters had taken. Daughter Diane remembers, 'Growing up, we didn't go without but we rarely had family holidays because racing was a seven day a week job, especially during the carnivals'.

In Hawaii, Pat and Chrissy noticed a line of people 50 metres long, going around the block, so they decided to see what all the fuss was about. 'The shop was selling pork ribs cooked in a BBQ sauce. There was nothing like it back in Australia.'

When Pat returned to Sydney, he talked to some friends about what he had seen in Hawaii. Were they interested in going to business with him?

'We found an old video shop for sale in Maroubra and turned it into a pork ribs joint. We fitted the whole shop beautifully, right down to the pink tiles to match the pork, all done by Chrissy of course.' The shop would be a takeaway outlet, so tables for eating were not required; but although they had a shop, they had no name and no product.

'We had trouble getting the ribs wholesale, so we had to pay top odds at $3.90 a kilo. We had the shop finished, the stock finalised and all the burners ready to go but we couldn't find the right BBQ sauce.'

Pat went to the nearest Campbell's Warehouse with good mate Dick Keats to search for a suitable rib sauce. 'We took the lids off and tried a few until we found the one that we liked. Dick was at one end of an aisle saying, "Up here, up here!" It tasted good so we took a couple of bottles with us and tried it on some ribs but it was too thick. We put it in a blender, added five parts water to two parts sauce and the ribs pretty much walked out the shop.'

When the shop added a chilli sauce to their menu, people were going through their garbage to see what sauce they were using. 'If only they knew,' Pat says, 'but we were buying it in bulk so I am sure the manufacturer was happy.'

They called the shop 'Arnold's Pork Ribs' and the place just took off. 'We couldn't think of a good name for the shop but then I remembered the 1960s TV show *Green Acres* with the pet pig, Arnold Ziffel, not even thinking about the connection with *Happy Days.*'

'We made a dollar out of it and then a bloke came along who wanted to franchise the business.' Soon, there were multiple Arnold's Ribs outlets around Sydney, ultimately adding pizza to the menu. 'But we made a bigger dollar out of the real estate.'

The next venture Pat and Chrissy entered into was a liquor store with jockey Denis McClune, who was riding for the stable at the time, and bookmaker Barry Cook. 'Les Edwards, a liquor distributor, was one of my owners and things weren't going that well at the stable and I was thinking of giving it away', he admits. Edwards talked Pat into the merits of a liquor store.

Pat scoured the local real estate guide looking for a suitable shop for sale and found one in a particular part of Maroubra. 'The Bronx!' Pat says. 'We didn't realise that the area was a known drug den and, even though the clientele wasn't great, we kept our margins tight on cartons and made our money on single bottles of beer.'

Because of Pat's busy training schedule, Chrissy was saddled with doing much of the shop work, he admits. 'I didn't want to leave her alone in the shop because it was potentially dangerous. The first day we were there, a guy was chased up the road on foot with two policemen, guns drawn, shouting "Stop! Stop!" I thought: hello, this is nice.'

Pat and Chrissy had a terrible time with shoplifters before getting the locals on side. 'Teenagers and drug addicts would run in while Chrissy was distracted out the back and grab a bottle of scotch and run for it', he says. The best way to get the locals on board was to befriend them and give them work.

'When the delivery truck came in from the brewery, we couldn't afford a forklift so we paid the locals to unpack the truck. They used to come into the shop and ask when the next delivery was arriving because they wanted the work. They became very protective of the business, and of Chrissy, who was like a mum to them.'

'They stood guard at the front of the shop and no one bothered us, not even the local drug addicts. The shop was now off limits.'

Pat also trained a horse for the boss of TNT Transport Group and the company did all their Christmas stock through the liquor store. 'We bought a livestock truck, with no power steering, and loaded it full of our product to make the deliveries.'

The hours were long and the work was hard, especially for Chrissy who worked Christmas Eve on several occasions while tending to the needs of her own family. 'We did that for abought three or four years before selling the shop to this wonderful gay couple who were very successful and ended up winning bottle shop of the year.'

Pat and Chrissy say they didn't make much money out of their ventures by the time they paid all the business tax, but it was another source of income and kept the family going when the horses weren't winning. 'It kept us motivated to get ahead,' Pat says, 'to build something from nothing'.

About that time, Pat was also part of a syndicate that included fellow trainer

Betty Lane, which put in a bid for the Doncaster Hotel in Kensington. 'Probably every bushy's dream is being a publican,' Pat says, 'or even better, marry the daughter of a publican'.

Pat could see the potential, but the syndicate fell agonisingly short – 'about $50,000,' Pat recalls, in a multi-million-dollar bid. 'I was prepared to sell everything to make it work, but some members of the syndicate got cold feet.'

Dick Thornett, the former first grade rugby league player and triple Australian 'rep' (rugby league, rugby union and rowing) was the owner of the Doncaster at the time. 'Dick was a lovely bloke but a terrible businessman,' Pat says, 'and it would have been easy to turn it around but it was not to be. In the end one of my owners bought it.'

He shudders to think what it is worth now. 'What could have been', he says.

CHAPTER 12

The Grey on the Hill

In the autumn of 1994, Pat thought he had finally found the good horse he was looking for. Ron Towell, who ran the GT Spelling Parks at Kulnura after buying it from the Websters' friends, Julie and Allan Putland, had bred a Bellotto colt from his mare Hanina. Pat was still spelling his horses there and Towell gave the gelding to Pat to train.

Montana Sands, '15 hands tall with a new pair of shoes on', recalls Pat, was knocked about in his first unplaced run at Hawkesbury, but there was a touch of class about the pocket rocket. At his second start, Montana Sands staged a remarkable performance in the Todman Slipper Trial (1200m). Starting at 140/1, the gelding missed the kick by six lengths before storming home to split Paulliac and Danzero in the run to the finish line.

Montana Sands wasn't entered in the Golden Slipper (1200m), AJC Sires Produce Stakes (1400m) or the Champagne Stakes (1600m) because training setbacks put the horse's preparation behind schedule. Pat resisted the temptation to pay huge late fees to secure a place in the top two-year-old races, and when the horse was 'a moral beaten' in the final qualifying race for the Slipper, the trainer sent the horse for a spell rather than run the precocious two year-old on three consecutive weekends.

'Danzero won the Slipper, and Montana Sands had beaten it home in the Todman', Pat laments.

Pat's knowledge of and care for his horses has always been second to none. As a result, the tiny two-year-old with a big heart raced on until he was an eight-year-old, winning nine races and amassing over $330,000 in prizemoney.

'And the only reason the horse was able to do that was because we looked after him', Pat says. But the owners needed to be patient. And Pat was the boss.

When the Geiger Counter colt Jebu won a modest $5000 maiden at Hawkesbury in 1997, Pat once again asked himself: is this my good horse? 'Jebu was a real handful. He was "head shy" – he went berserk when you went near him with a bridle and it took him an hour to get ready for work', Pat says.

At Jebu's second race appearance, the highly-strung gelding was withdrawn at the barrier and stewards ordered him to trial after refusing to go into the stalls. Jebu then came out and blitzed a good field at his next start. At his third start, Jebu dead-headed with the prophetically-named Son and Heir, and from there his promising career was all but over. Jebu was a bad bleeder, and the horse was sent to America to race.

Pat never gets ahead of himself when he finds a promising horse. 'The owners do that', he says.

Century's Haul was only a handy horse, winning four races and $88,000 in prizemoney in the early 1990s. There is little space for sentiment in sport, but Pat was emotional after winning the Melanoma Cup at Kembla Grange with his gelding. An initiative of the NSW Cancer Council, the sponsorship of the race was designed to raise awareness of the scourge of melanoma.

'I lost both my parents to cancer', he told pressmen. 'I think about them all the time.'

Pats parents are buried in Dubbo, and there is a part of him that always wanted to return to the bush. 'We had saved some money and thought about buying a place in the country,' he says. 'A mate of mine, Johnny Quinlan, lived at Mudgee at the time and we thought we'd go up and have a beer with him and see if there was anything suitable for sale.'

The Websters went into the local Richardson & Wrench real estate office and asked the woman at reception if there was any acreage for sale. Helen Woods, who ran the agency with her husband Dennis, would become close friends with Pat and Chrissy.

The agency had just placed a suitable property on their books, but it wasn't for sale yet. 'It may be too much for you', Helen said, but she showed them a prospectus anyway. The property was about 17 km outside town on the Gulgong Road next too Goree Stud. It was called 'Belinfante.'

The real estate agent rang the property's owner Bill Poulton and arranged for her husband Dennis to take Pat and Chrissy out there the following day. 'That night at the Red Heifer pub over a few beers, we looked at the price and asked ourselves if it was worth it. We had a look the next day and Chrissy fell in love with the place.'

The actual homestead was made out of rock found on the property and hand-carved by stonemasons who came all the way from Adelaide to complete the job. The Websters learned that the property received its name after a tragedy at the turn of the previous century. There was a small bridge leading into Wellington, and the story goes that a French doctor came out during a storm to deliver a baby on the property and drowned when he was swept off the bridge. Belinfante is Spanish for 'beautiful child'.

'When we were at the property, there was a grey horse standing under a tree. My mate Dick Keats was with us and said to Bill, "What's that horse over there?" It was a yearling by Spectacular Spy out of a mare called Zemelda.'

'Dick said to Bill, "If you still want the full price why don't you throw in the horse with the sale of the place?" Bill was a blueblood – we were common folk and he was gentry. "No, no", he said. He owned the mother and wanted to race the horse himself'.

They settled on a price on the condition that Pat got the horse to train. 'Bill said we could lease it from him and he would come into the racing partnership. Dennis Woods piped up that he would come into it as well.'

The unraced grey was named Ab Initio, which is a Latin term used in law which means 'in the beginning'.

When Pat trialled the colt, it didn't show much interest in racing so he suggested that it be gelded. 'I worked Ab Initio with Jebu, who was the star of the stable at the time, and it went pretty well.' Danny Beasley rode Ab Initio in his race debut at Newcastle and he duly saluted at 6/1.

As with all his horses, Pat took a patient route with Ab Initio, spacing his runs and bringing him through his grades. The gelding won five races before the stable set it for the Group 2 Challenge Stakes first up at Randwick in January 1999. Ridden by Larry Cassidy, Ab Initio sat three and four wide for the trip before being sooled to the front to win by almost three lengths. It was an effortless win.

Ab Initio, 'the grey flash', had arrived. It was Pat's second Group 2 success, coming a full decade after At Sea's win in the same race.

The following month, the four-year-old lined up in the Group 3 Frederick Clissold Stakes (1200m). Ab Initio defeated Landsighting and Little Lucifer, with the well-fancied Adam a close fourth. 'When Ab Initio won the Frederick Clissold with Glen Boss on top, we were driving home from Rosehill', says Pat. 'Wayne was so happy the horse had won, he was crying in the back seat of the car. That's how much it meant to us. He asked if we could stop at the nearest service station for a piddle and I drove off on him. It was a very happy time for the stable.'

The real test would be the Group 1 Galaxy Stakes (1100m) in April, but Ab Initio struck a heavy track. Pat's grey ran a creditable fourth behind Masked Party, Notoire and Rebel Rock. 'Interestingly, the three place-getters in the Galaxy ran three lasts at their next starts.'

At his next start, Ab Initio proved his class by winning the Group 3 TJ Smith Stakes (1200m). 'It was an honour to win that race, because I admired TJ so much.' The Hall of Fame trainer had passed away the previous year, aged eighty-two. Unfortunately for Pat and the connections, the race would not be promoted to a Group 1 event until 2005, with a large dollop of prizemoney added.

Pat took Ab Initio to the Brisbane Carnival in May 1999, but after running a good third to Staging in the Group 3 Carlton Cup (1200m), the gelding finished down the track in the Group 1 Doomben 10,000 (1350m). The horse had had enough racing for the time being and was sent for a spell.

Ab initio won the Group 3 The Shorts in Spring of 1999, turning the tables on the good mare Staging. Ab Initio was Pat Webster's first home-grown group horse – he had inherited At Sea as a proven group performer but had found his grey standing on a hill up in Mudgee. Although that elusive Group 1 victory would elude him for some time yet, Pat won more individual races with Ab Initio that with any other horse in his stable – thirteen races in all – and collected over $600,000 in stakes money.

Returning from a spell, the now five-year-old started favourite in the Group 2 Challenge Stakes (1000m) in February 2000, but was beaten by Easy Rocking, trained by Pat's good mate Ron Quinton. Ab Initio's form tapered off badly that autumn, with four unplaced runs in Melbourne and Sydney before the gelding lined up in its second straight TJ Smith Stakes.

Before the race, Pat learned that the managing owners were planning to transfer Ab Initio to the John Hawkes stable at the end of his current preparation. If that was true, it would be disappointing. Ab Initio was the best horse Pat had, and good horses only came along every decade or so.

Pat also had another runner in the TJ Smith Stakes, the moderately performed Shy Hero. 'I liked him as a yearling but he cost too much – about $90,000 from memory', Pat says. 'Then I saw him in a breeze up sale where horses are worked over the last furlong and I liked what I saw. I got talking to bloodstock agent Nick Vass, who I had met at the races when Ab Initio started winning, and so we bought Shy Hero then.'

Shy Hero won at the provincials and Vass thought the horse had a lot of potential. 'It was crazy running a Class 1 horse in a group race, but Nick was keen to see what Shy Hero could do in the city.'

The other part of the Shy Hero story is apprentice jockey Jackson Morris. 'I was at the races one day and trainer Allan Denham said to me, "Pat, my apprentice is riding in the last. Can I put him under your care because I need to go home?" Good as gold, I said, because apprentice jockeys have to be in the care of a senior trainer on race day and I was happy to help out.

'I went to the jockey's room and asked if I could see Jackson Morrison for a moment. "Yes Mr Webster?" he asks. "Allan Denham has left you in my charge – and call me Pat." "Yes sir", he replied. What a nice kid, I thought.'

Jackson Morris is an enigma, a talented rider who has battled his own self-destructive tendencies to make comeback after comeback to racing. Apprenticed to John Hawkes, the country hoop transferred to Allan Denham and rode in a lot of provincial races for Allan and his taciturn father, Jack.

'Jackson was working really hard for me so I gave him a couple of rides on my horses. Because Shy Hero was a Class 1 horse, I was struggling to find a rider for the TJ Smith so I put Jackson on it, a 3kg-claiming apprentice in a no-claiming race.' Just like Pat was when he won his first race at Randwick on Medieval Marvel all those years ago.

Pat told his young jockey to find the fence on Shy Hero and bring the horse home. In the run, Morris somehow found himself trapped three and four wide after jumping from barrier 4. Watching the race on track, Pat shook his head in disgust. The young apprentice was looking at a kick up the arse instead of a slap on the back upon his return to scale. Holding the horse together, however, Morris got Shy Hero to stick his neck out right on the line and defeated favourite Easy Rocking at odds of $58 on the tote.

It was Pat's second successive win in the TJ Smith Stakes, but with arguably the wrong horse. Ab Initio finished seventh. 'The grey was always a little fragile, and then he bled after the 2000 TJ Smith. The swab attendant who hosed him down after the race noticed him bleeding from the nostrils. I rang Dennis Woods with the bad news, and when I was at Canterbury Races the following day, I let chief steward Ray Murrihy know.'

It was an automatic three-month ban for the gelding. Then all hell broke loose.

'Some members of the syndicate said that because I heard they were going to take the horse off me I had made the bleeding attack up out of spite', Pat says, still angry at the insult. 'Ray Murrihy opened an inquiry that went on and on; there was no need for it because the girl in the hosing dock had witnessed the bleeding attack.'

The inquiry went for a day and a half with no result. Murrihy asked if Pat had told any members of the syndicate about the bleeding attack. It was then Pat remembered that he had phoned Dennis Woods to let him know, and he had the phone records to back it up. Midway through the second day, Pat gave the stewards a copy of the phone records and a signed statutory declaration detailing their conversation.

'Murrihy asked why didn't I give them this in the first place? "That's easy", I said. I didn't have it then!'

But the end was result was still the same. Pat still lost the horse to John Hawkes. 'Dennis Woods stuck solid with me and asked me what he should do. In the end he decided to sell his share in the horse.'

Pat had been in the racing game long enough to know that losing a good horse is part and parcel of the sport. 'You start off with a lot of goodwill, you win races, and then it goes sour. The owners just couldn't understand why I told stewards the horse had bled. Some trainers might turn a blind eye, but I couldn't.'

'What if I put a kid on Ab Initio like Chrissy's nephew Jason Lee, and the horse collapsed in a race and he was injured or killed?' he asks. 'I couldn't live with myself.'

Ab Initio only won one more race during his career, winning a second Frederick Clissold Stakes for John Hawkes in 2001, but was plagued by the same issues Pat had dealt with as his trainer.

'Just because they get the horse doesn't mean they get the training recipe', Pat says with a wry smile.

When Pat and Chrissy Webster purchased Belinfante at Mudgee in the mid-1990s, the plan was to live there and have son Wayne operate the Randwick stables. The arrival of Patrick's son Jack in 1999, and the Websters' decision to raise him as their own, meant they couldn't get away to Mudgee as often as they liked to.

'It wasn't fair on Jack to be shooting off to Mudgee every weekend', says Pat. 'There was a swimming pool and tennis court there, but he was too young to enjoy them. Once he started school, we obviously needed to be in the city so we decided to sell the property in Mudgee.'

Pat and Chrissy entrusted the sale of the homestead to their good friends Helen and Dennis Woods, and the property was snapped up by a corporate lawyer from England.

'After we sold Mudgee, we bought an investment terrace at Randwick', Pat says. 'Chrissy said she always wanted to live in a Sydney terrace with lots of fireplaces but after we bought it, she didn't want to live there because she was spoilt for space living in the family home at Eastern Avenue.' They decided to keep the terrace house as a rental property.

'Then Eastern Avenue got a bit big for us; the kids moved out so we decided to sell up and buy somewhere rural. For the next five years we looked and looked everywhere. Although we had been friends with the team from GT Spelling paddocks at Kulnura, we didn't even look there until a property came on the market.'

Pat and Chrissy decided to have a look at a farm that was recommended to them at Mangrove Mountain. Formally known as Antler Farm, the 58-acre property had a homestead, tennis court and swimming pool. 'Chrissy said she wouldn't live there if my life depended on it!' Pat laughs. 'We missed out on another property at Kiama – and probably lucky that we did – so we had another look at the Central Coast. I could see the potential here, although there was no grass in the paddocks.'

Corporate investor Russell Goward had poured millions into the property in the 1990s, turning it into the largest deer farm in the country. The farm was repossessed by the National Australia Bank, the largest of Goward's creditors, when the Sydney businessman went to gaol for two years for making false statements about his share trading.

But Pat was taken with the property. 'I said to Chrissy: you do the negotiation, but don't stuff it up.' Chrissy agreed as long as she got a new kitchen for the homestead. 'Done,' said Pat.

Pat and Chrissy have lived at Kulnura now for the past ten years. 'We run enough cattle on the property during the year to cover the land and water rates. And it keeps the grass down on the paddocks.'

The property also has a large guest shed – beautifully fitted out – where Patrick Jnr lives, with extra sleeping quarters for those who need to get away from the worries of the city. A creek runs through property, and Pat takes jockeys battling addiction down to the weir where they can open up about their problems.

For Pat and Chrissy, home is where the heart is.

CHAPTER 13

A Horse Called God

On Boxing Day 2007, Pat trained a rare city double on the Randwick Kensington track. A little after Pampas won a BM64 handicap, Mizone saluted at good odds in a BM76. Mizone had struggled to win a maiden at Cessnock at his 15th start in a race, but later went on to win a Frank Underwood Cup and almost $200,000 in prizemoney.

Speaking to journos after the win, Pat gave credit to son Wayne, who had taken on the role of his stable foreman. The veteran horseman took the opportunity to once again push for the introduction of training partnerships, as was allowed in other states, but resisted by NSW Racing authorities at the time.

'A son can win a grand final, but his father isn't part of it,' Pat told the press. 'To share in a partnership-like training is different.'

Wayne Webster had become an integral part of Pat's training setup at Randwick. Wayne had grown up around the stable – Pat used to allow him to feed the horses at the age of six, 'the slow ones, anyway,' he says – but Pat and Chrissy wanted each of their children to find a trade away from racing. Wayne left school at age sixteen and started a chef's apprenticeship. He took over as Pat's stable foreman from older brother Patrick, who was again going through a period of personal difficulty.

'Patrick was good with horses and loved the life', says Pat. 'Wayne got thrown into it.' Theirs would be the first training partnership registered in NSW.

On 1 August 2008, Racing NSW finally relented. Training partnerships would give young trainers a foot in the door without having to start out from scratch, the combination of fresh ideas and old-world experience having the potential to rejuvenate the sport. But in Pat and Wayne's case, there was an added bond. Father and son.

And Wayne was grateful for the opportunity – not only to train in his own right, but also to work with his dad, but he was under no illusion that it would be easy.

Pat was a hard taskmaster. 'I can't replace you as a son, but I will replace you as a worker', he told Wayne. 'Let's get that straight. Everyone's replaceable.'

Wayne understood what his father was saying. 'If you got on the wrong side of him, he would give you life and one week', Wayne laughs.

Wayne's promotion to co-trainer, though, was just reward for his unsung efforts over many years. There were many horses in the stable that Wayne took full care of, but only Pat's name as trainer was in the race book. 'Mizone was a perfect example of that, so was Parfumier and Shy Hero. Wayne loved Shy Hero, and not just because he backed it when it won the TJ Smith Stakes at 50/1'.

The training partnership came at the best and worst of times. The stable had fallen to no more than a dozen horses, but now the Webster partnership could build the team up to at least twenty. This was still far short of the ideal number of horses for a training partnership, which was about thirty to forty horses, but Pat always had a good strike rate with his team. In the season immediately before the training partnership began, Pat and Wayne had a phenomenal eighteen winners and twenty placings from just over 100 starters.

But there was a perfect storm brewing from the moment training partnerships came into being. First, the outbreak of equine influenza seriously stymied racing in NSW and then all Randwick trainers were relocated to Warwick Farm when racing headquarters was being utilised for the World Youth Day visit from Pope Benedict XVI.

'We were heavily compensated for the move, so I wish the Pope would come out here again,' Pat observes, 'but it was a pain in the arse, really. And my car was broken into twice while I was out at Warwick Farm'.

One of the first horses the Websters sent to the races in partnership was called Heza Kool Kat. In an ominous sign, the horse was killed when it knocked its head on the barrier before a race at Kembla Grange. Pat was understandably upset, complaining to stewards that the horse had been left in the barrier far too long.

'The owner pays the bills for three years with no result', he lamented.

The first official winner Pat and Wayne Webster co-trained was Luctonian. Then the winners inexplicably dried up. The stable didn't win a race for nine months until Thankgodyou'rehere came along.

'When photo finishes don't go your way and things get tough, people start to look at you and go, "Geez, you haven't had a winner for a while"', Pat said at the time. He tried to keep stable morale up, because the lack of winners can be so disheartening.

But Pat and Wayne refused to rush things. 'It's not how many times you run the horse but how many times you can win with them', Wayne told the press. Pat had said the same thing many times of the lean years.

Then Parfumier won, and Spanish King saluted at Hawkesbury. The Gerry Harvey-owned Parfumier later ran second in the 2009 Villiers Stakes – a race that would play a big part in Pat's later success with Happy Clapper.

'Parfumier is the king of our stable and he lets every horse in the place know it', Wayne observed. Parfumier was sent to Singapore, where it won first up at 33/1 with John Meagher as trainer. He won another ten races in Singapore and raced on as a ten-year-old. 'Wayne said Parfumier was the closest thing to a human being he has come across in a horse,'

Pat's brothers in law, Jim and Greg Lee, had also been granted a racing partnership but in 2010 the Lees were banned for five months after a test for sodium bicarbonate or 'milkshakes' as they were popularly known –

once a common practice, now outlawed – came back positive.

Pat took over all twenty-three horses in the Lees' stable for the five months, opting to use the fawn colours he inherited from Tiger Holland on their runners rather than his own orange and black colours. At its first run for Pat, Keeping The Dream won the Group 3 Gosford Cup at $41 with young jockey Tommy Berry in the saddle. In his acceptance speech, Pat modestly gave all credit to the win to his brothers-in-law.

In a nice touch, Nathan Berry substituted for twin brother Tommy in claiming the winning jockey's trophy. No one on course, especially Pat, was any the wiser. Tragically, Nathan Berry would succumb to a virus after falling ill in Singapore in 2014, aged just 24.

The Webster stable hit another level of success altogether, however, with the arrival of Thankgodyou'rehere. In 2008, Pat received a phone call from Canberra owner-breeder and former bookmaker Michael Thomas. 'I have a two-year-old horse for you', Pat recalls Michael telling him.

'No-one has rung for years offering me a new horse', was the trainer's blunt response.

Michael Thomas had worked for a year at the AJC offices at Randwick in 1979 and had met Pat, briefly sharing an elevator lift, so he knew who he was and had a 'good feel' for him as a trainer. 'The main reason for giving Thankgodyou'rehere to Pat was my horses were being trained by Matt Dale in Canberra and Matt wanted to take a year off and follow his heart travelling', Thomas recalls.

'Matt Dale trained Gunfire Messiah, Thankgodyou'rehere's older brother, and that horse was sent to Peter Morgan in Melbourne because he had a water walker and that suited his needs', Thomas says. 'I said to Matty, "What are we going to do about 'God?'"'

'God' was the stable name they gave to Thankgodyou'rehere, the last of the progeny from Thomas' gun mare, Winifred's Prayer. 'Well, it's not like we could call him "Thank" or "You'rehere"', Michael says. The Secret Savings two-year-old was named after the popular theatre sports show on TV at the time.

Dale and Thomas threw a couple trainers' names around, but they both decided a 'non-factory trainer' at Randwick would be ideal, although the choices were limited – Les Bridge, Kevin Moses, Ron Quinton or Pat Webster.

'I asked (trainer) John O'Shea, if he was going to give the horse to anyone at Randwick, who would he pick? He said, "What about Pat Webster?" and that was that.'

Thankgodyou'rehere trialled for Pat at Warwick Farm with Mitchell Bell riding. 'The horse finished sixth or seventh, and Mitchell hopped off and said, "I think you have a Group horse here." I thought, bloody hell! He finished down the track'.

Pat though the horse a 'beautiful colt, talented but injury prone. He went shin sore five times in the same leg! If someone left a match on the ground, he'd fall over it'.

'God' finally made his debut in April 2009 as a late three-year-old. 'We took him to Gosford with Corey Brown on top, and Thankgodyou'rehere started $2.25 favourite. It was a heavy track, which he didn't like, but the horse just didn't try. I rang Michael and suggested we geld the horse.'

Thankgodyou'rehere came out the following month and broke his maiden at Gosford at his second race start. Like all of Pat's horses, 'God' didn't take a lot of work to get fit … 'just enough to have him ticking over', he says. 'He always raced best fresh.'

This race also saw the beginning of the horse's association with rider Rodney Quinn. 'Rodney Quinn was the "King of Kembla", a very good rider but, more importantly, a gentleman and one of the nicest men you'll ever meet. He was also a great mentor to Wayne as a young trainer, especially in being able to tell him how horses pull up and what distance they were looking for.'

Thankgodyou'rehere came back to racing in his four-year-old season in great form, winning five races and running two seconds. 'Michael Thomas is a big believer in putting a horse through his classes', Pat says. The best of these wins was in the Group 3 Hawkesbury Gold Cup over 1600m in November 2010.

'Could he run a mile? Could he handle the soft conditions? There were a lot of questions.' Thankgodyou'rehere sustained a long run in his first try at Group level and beat Glintz by a half neck with Kimillsey a nose away third. Pat couldn't see the finish of the race from where he was watching on course, but he looked across to see son Wayne jumping in the air excitedly, so he knew the horse had won.

Pat views this victory as the highlight of his career to this point because he achieved a rare Group win with his youngest son as co-trainer. Wayne was particularly bullish after the win. 'Give me a good 3 track at Randwick and 1400m and I'd race him against any horse is Australia.'

Thankgodyou'rehere was then sent for a spell and set for the Group 1 Galaxy first up in April 2011. The race has remained something of a bogey race for Pat. It had been twelve years since he saddled up speed machine Ab Initio in the race. The grey started a warm favourite but finished fourth on a heavy track and, not for the first time, the weather gods were against him. The heavens opened and Randwick produced a bog track on the day of the race.

Try as he might, 'God' could not reel in the mudlark Atomic Force. Pat's gelding finished second. 'It was a huge run,' Pat maintains. 'The wet track was the difference between winning and losing with him.'

In a bitter postscript to the race, Atomic Force's trainer David Smith was later suspended for fifteen years for administering the banned substance cobalt to his horses. 'It leaves a sour taste in your mouth', Pat says all these years later, on losing a Group 1 to a proven drug cheat. 'I don't mind trainers trying to get an edge, but you have to operate on a level playing field.'

A HORSE CALLED GOD

Pat aimed Thankgodyou'rehere for the Brisbane Winter Carnival, and although the gelding ran good races in the Listed Prime Minister's Cup (1300m), Darley BRC Sprint (1350m) and Stradbroke Handicap (1400m), the gelding failed to win in Brisbane.

Returning in the spring, Thankgodyou'rehere was primed to return in the Listed Show County Quality (1200m) at Warwick Farm in August 2011. The only minor complication was Pat and Chrissy's daughter Diane was being married in Cairns on the day before the horse's return. Pat and Wayne readied their horses for their weekend assignments and then flew to Cairns on the morning of the wedding. Only they went to the wrong resort.

'Who knew there was more than one Palm Cove resort in Cairns?' Pat says. Arriving in time to walk his daughter down the aisle, Pat and family celebrated in style before finding a bar that showed the races coverage the following day.

Thankgodyou'rehere finished unplaced on a heavy track first up. 'The attendant behind the barrier put his hand up to signal the starter and Rodney Quinn wasn't even in the saddle', Pat says. 'He was standing on the side and only had one foot in the stirrups.' More bad luck.

A good win in the Group 3 Tramway Stakes (1400m) primed Thankgodyou'rehere for a tilt at the Group 1 Epsom Handicap (1600m). Pat was so nervous about running in the Group 1 race he couldn't bear to check the final barrier draw so he rang a friend in Sydney and asked, 'Are you going to tell me the good news or the bad news?'

There was a short pause. The horse drew barrier 2.

'A barrier can be the difference between winning and losing, so anywhere between 2 and 6 is perfect in a big field', Pat says. 'With lightweight jockey, Rod Quinn could have "God" handily placed to the turn and challenging in the straight.'

Instead, a disaster. Thankgodyou'rehere knocked his head in the barriers. 'Rod Quinn said the horse lunged at the gates before they opened and was dazed in the run. I was watching the start of the race on a TV monitor in a quiet corner on track like I always do, and I clearly heard a God-almighty thump as his head hit the barrier stall.'

'God' dropped out and ran second last. Another opportunity gone.

Spacing his runs to keep the horse fresh, Thankgodyou'rehere lined up in the Group 3 TAB.com.au Stakes (1400m) at Flemington on Derby Day three weeks later. Ridden by premier Melbourne jockey Damien Oliver, Thankgodyou'rehere ran a two length second to the good Queensland sprinter Woorim.

The gelding only spent three weeks in the paddock, but wasn't quite right in the autumn of 2012. 'The horse has a motor of a V8 Supercar but hasn't got the body to cope with it. I had to give him enough work without doing too much and that was the hard part. Even as a six-year-old, he had only raced on twenty occasions. A big stable wouldn't have persevered with him.'

After a fair fifth in the Group 1 Galaxy (1200m), Pat wasn't that keen to take the horse to Brisbane that year. 'He got knocked around as a beaten favourite in the Prime Ministers Cup and drew barrier 16 in the Stradbroke Handicap and was never a chance.'

After a disappointing campaign with the gelding, Pat was informed that the horse was going to Peter Morgan at Whittlesea in Melbourne. 'Peter Morgan, who Michael had known for many years, was one of the first trainers to have a water walker for his horses. Thankgodyou'rehere had leg issues and Michael thought he would be better off sending the horse there.'

'I'm not a stable jumper by any means,' says Michael Thomas, 'but it was apparent the horse needed those facilities. "God" was going off the boil so I decided to send him to Peter Morgan. Pat was unhappy about it, but I wasn't going anywhere … just shuffling my horses around'.

Thankgodyou'rehere only raced three more times in Melbourne but did not improve on his winning record. 'I was watching the gallops on Sky Channel and he was in a big race at Mooney Valley (Moir Stakes). I saw

Above: Pat Webster, age 13, as an apprentice jockey in Betty Lane and 'Tiger' Holland's stable in Geurie, NSW. (Courtesy Webster family)

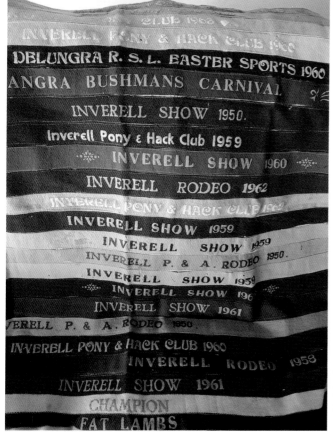

Pat's many Show jumping ribbons, lovingly made into a blanket by his late mother, Blanche. (Courtesy Webster family)

As an apprentice jockey in 1967, having won on Murky Night at Randwick. (Courtesy Webster family)

Below: Pat's win on Golden Draw in the 1966 Parkes Cup. 'I walked onto the track not even having a ride in the race.' (Courtesy Webster family)

Mr. P. Pike's g.a. "*Golden Draw*" (Faux Trigo - Golden Chime) 7st. 7lbs. JOHN BEGG
10 furlongs
R. Moson   Jockey P. Webster   Shivoo 2nd Pinkenbah 3rd   Time 2-6⅖   Margins 1½ len.-2

London Rep, backed from 100/1 to 12's, salutes at Canterbury Park with Pat Webster in the saddle. (Courtesy Webster family)

Pat Webster weighs in after winning on London Rep in June 1967. 'I had no idea they had backed it.' (Courtesy Webster family)

Having turned to training, Pat unsaddles a winner ridden by jockey Noel Barker in 1979. Barker was tragically killed in a barrier trial accident the following year. (Courtesy Webster family)

Sail to Success, ridden by Shane Arnold, sporting Pat's stable colours of orange with black Maltese cross and armbands. 'Do you know how to make a Maltese cross?' (Courtesy Webster family, artwork by Andrew Davies)

Pat with stable apprentice Shane Arnold and 'Cocky' Webster at his Randwick stables in the 1980s. (Courtesy Webster family)

Pat Webster took maidens to the provincials for decades before getting his first Group horse, At Sea. (Courtesy Webster family)

Pat at the Inglis & Sons yearling sales in the 1990s. 'The most persistent underbidder in racing.' (Courtesy Webster family)

Pat and Chrissy's three children, (from top), Wayne, Diane and Patrick, in the late 1990s. (Courtesy Webster family)

Happy Clapper surges to the post to win the 2017 Epsom Handicap. It was Pat Webster's first win at Group 1 level as a trainer. (Courtesy AAP)

Happy Clapper wins the Group 1 Canterbury Stakes first up at Randwick in 2018. (Courtesy AAP)

Stunning photographic portraits of
Happy Clapper by Sarah Ebbett.
(Courtesy Sarah Ebbett Photography)

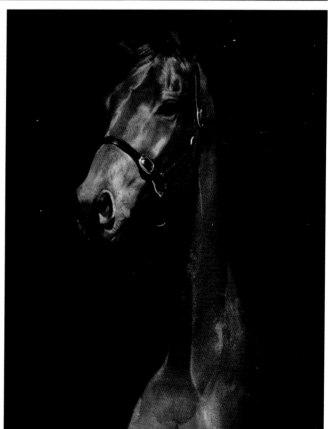

Above: Happy Clapper wins the 2018 Doncaster Mile after running second on two previous occasions. (Courtesy AAP)

Pat's trainer's trophy for training the 2018 Doncaster Mile winner. The beautiful diamond and jade encrusted trophy was given to the Websters' daughter, Diane. (Photo by Alan Whiticker)

Left: Happy Clapper parades at Randwick wearing his pre-race red ear muffs. (Photo by Alan Whiticker)

Below: 'Super Mare' Winx relegates Happy Clapper to second place in the 2019 Apollo Stakes in February 2019. The pair met 11 times at Group 1 level, with the Clapper running second to her five times. (Photo by Alan Whiticker)

Trainer Pat Webster confers with Happy Clapper's jockey Blake Shinn before the running of the All-Star Mile at Flemington in April 2019. (Photo by Alan Whiticker)

Happy Clapper 'star' on the Flemington Racecourse walkway before the inaugural All Star Mile. (Photo by Alan Whiticker)

HAPPY CLAPPER

THE ALL-STAR MILE

Happy Clapper, led by strapper and regular trackwork rider Ainsley Fox, enters the Flemington enclosure. (Photo by Alan Whiticker)

Pat, where he's happiest ... on the family farm at Kulnura on the NSW Central Coast, deep in thought. (Courtesy Diane Webster)

him galloping in his trackwork with other horses over 1000m and I though the horse was in trouble then. He wasn't a horse that could work with other horses.'

The gelding finished third behind Buffering in the Moir Stakes (1200m), and after an unplaced run at Caulfield, finished his career with a fourth in the Heffernan Stakes (1300m) at Sandown. 'He was an unlucky horse and could have won a couple of Group 1s, but we just kept beating our head against the wall with him'.

The great irony is, after his racing career Thankgodyou'rehere ended back at the Webster's farm at Kulnura. 'The old gelding leads a life of luxury up here with another former racehorse we have named Deedee Flyer. They just run the show up here. Horses are herd animals, and they chase the cows around the paddock like they own the place. They get hay every day and the odd carrot ..."

'Yes, "God's" been good to us', he smiles.

And Happy Clapper was just around the corner.

CHAPTER 14

The Gentle Giant

When Happy Clapper came into Pat and Wayne Webster's stable in 2012, they were still taking maidens to the provincials, searching for that elusive good horse. That has always been part of the romance of racing, Pat says – but so has the blood, sweat and tears shed worrying about what fate has in store for each horse in his stable.

Enter a tall, gangly animal, still growing into his giant frame of 17 hands, with a head as big as a phone box. 'The Clapper' as he became known around the stable, was trouble from the start.

'We just had so much drama with the horse. I don't know if he was broken in properly or not, but when I got him the horse always wanted to hang out badly.'

Fortunately, Pat and Wayne had a great team behind them to help with Happy Clapper. 'It's a small team and we've all been so dedicated', he says. 'Paul Sempf was apprenticed to me at an early age. He got homesick for the Gold Coast but he ended coming back to us and working in the stable as a trackwork rider. He really is an exceptional horseman and he put so much time into Clapper.'

The first issue was to solve the horse's tendency to 'hang out' under pressure, turning its head outwards when straightening and running off the track. 'We'd work Clapper with another horse deliberately to teach him not to hang out. This was on the Randwick B track, which is circular, and Pauly would bring Clapper inside the other horse as he came into the turn. That pretty much fixed that.'

Track rider, New Zealander Ainsley Fox, was another important piece of the puzzle. Fox spent four years as a trackwork rider and strapper for the Lee brothers, but when they scaled down their stable Pat Webster quickly moved to hire her. 'Without Ainsley there would not be any Clapper,' he says, 'Her sectional times on him are to perfection.'

Fox and the Clapper formed a special bond. 'He'll hear me come in of a morning, stand at the front of his box and wait', Fox told journalist Brad Gray in 2019. 'Butter wouldn't melt in his mouth. He knows his routine and loves it. He is an absolute gentleman on the ground but not so much to ride. He is very strong and loves to gallop.'

Fox spent three years with the Webster stable before they too decided to downsize. Pat still wanted Ainsley to ride Clapper, despite her now working full-time for Anthony Cummings. Ainsley rides him every morning and straps him on race day.

Fox has seen a lot of changes with the horse. She's been there since the beginning, when he was flighty and immature. Before his first tilt at the Doncaster, Happy Clapper threw Ainsley in trackwork, after shying at blades of grass that were moving with the wind, and took off without her. The addition of large red earmuffs before a race has filtered out much of the extraneous noise of the parade ring.

'Before he wore ear muffs he used to shy at everything', she says.

'I've gone out to see him spelling in the paddock and as soon as I hopped over the fence he came running over', Fox said recently. 'He followed me everywhere. I sat down and he had his head in my lap. He is about 17 hands but a gentle giant … (and) if he doesn't get worked, he knows he is racing that day too. He's a smart horse.'

Pat has thanked Ainsley Fox on numerous occasions after the horse's big race wins, but many past and present employees have had a role to play in making him the horse he is today. No more than stable foreman John Burke who has been at the stable since the day Happy Clapper arrived.

John Burke is a former detective chief inspector and acting superintendent of police who started turning up at the Randwick stables on his day off, doing odd jobs and feeding the horses. 'John was a "hard nut" as a cop', Pat says. 'Interestingly, he knew my father from their days drinking at the Courthouse Hotel in the city. Imagine that, a cop and a painter and docker getting along!'

The first day John Burke turned up at trackwork, Pat recalls that he was wearing his police uniform. 'I had to ask him to come in his civvies next time because I was scared that half the trackwork riders at Randwick would run for the hills when they saw him in his police gear.'

When John Burke retired in the 1990s, he retreated to his property in Tamworth before making his way back to Pat's Randwick stables. After a time, he became stable foreman for Pat and Wayne.

'Pat keeps telling me he's only employing me to keep me alive,' John laughs when I met him at Pat's stables one afternoon after he finished working the horses, 'but he's a very dear friend, as is all the family. I appreciate the responsibility I have here and working with all the horses, but Happy Clapper is the best horse I'll ever have anything to do with. He's one of nature's gentlemen … a bit like myself!'

'Burkey' still remembers the day the gelding arrived at Pat's stable. 'He was standing in his box, this big, boof-headed thing, so I rang Pat at home. "That horse that came in overnight? It's huge. What's it by?" Pat said, "Teabags, or some bloody thing". We'd never heard of the sire, Teofilo, because Happy Clapper was from his first crop.'

Happy Clapper first took his place in a 740m trial at Randwick on 25 February 2013 on a soft 7 track. Jay Ford, the jockey who had ridden champion sprinter Takeover Target to success around the world, was the rider. Pat was not even on track after handing over the day-to-day running of the stable to son Wayne.

'We still didn't know if Clapper was any good until Jay Ford rode him in the trial. He finished fourth, a little over three lengths from the winner, but the track was damp and he wasn't altogether happy in the going. Jay rang me afterwards and said the horse was something special. We know now Clapper always trials really well first up, but that was certainly an eye-opener.'

After another trial the following month, a nice third over 1050m beaten just over a length, the team turned the horse out and sent him up to GT Spelling Park next to the Websters' farm.

'I told Michael Thomas that we should run the horse first up at Kembla Grange because it's a big track, just in case he hung out again. The horse wasn't really a betting proposition yet because we didn't know how good he was, so I suggested we put a girl jockey on him because she'll be kind to him and he won't get hurt. If he wins, he wins.'

But something in the back of his mind told the veteran trainer the horse was good … very good. 'I even told Chrissy that she should come to Kembla and watch the race because I thought we had a very good racehorse on our hands. Chrissy doesn't go to the races anymore because she gets too nervous.'

Hannah Martin was the young jockey who rode Happy Clapper out to the barriers in his first race start. Someone liked the horse's chances, because it firmed from $7.50 to $5.00, and second favourite. 'Clapper came out a little slow and the jockey got back, but he flew home and ran third behind a couple of handy horses.'

Team Webster put the horse out for another four weeks, before getting him ready for the races with a strong third in a 1060m trial behind emerging champion Fast 'n Rocking in August 2013. Jockey James McDonald was booked for the gelding's second start, with Wayne putting the finishing touches on the horse while Pat was away working for Racing NSW.

'I rushed home from Inverell to watch Clapper run at Rosehill and when he came out slow, James McDonald went early on him and the horse was run down and ran second. I still thought he was a good horse in the making.'

At his next start at Rosehill, Happy Clapper ran fourth with Tim Clarke up, beaten a little over a length in a blanket finish. 'I told the jockey to be patient on him but he took off at the 700m and that's why he got the sack. I still get on great with Tim, but I know it hurts him that Clapper went on to win all those races.'

The Spring Stakes (1600m) is a good three-year-old race during the Newcastle Cup carnival; a springboard to the Champion Stakes (2000m) and the VRC Derby (2500m) later in the spring. 'Teofilo was producing some good stayers, so the idea was to try Clapper over a distance. We thought he was a winning chance, but he only plodded to the line because he was still immature.'

After finishing third in a Group 3 race at just his fourth start, Pat opted to send the horse for another spell rather than press onward to the rich three-year-old races. 'Clapper was growing every day. Michael Thomas was a very patient owner. Every time I said I wanted to give Clapper a long break, he agreed.'

Happy Clapper came back to racing in the early months of 2014, the stable again using two trials to bring the gelding to race fitness. It was also the first time the horse raced in blinkers and utilised the skills of jockey Blake Shinn. Bookies posted the horse as odd-on favourite in the 3-year-old Maiden Plate (1400m) on Randwick's Kensington track but the horse ran second, beaten by a neck on a track that favoured leaders.

'I thought he was disappointing, and so did the owner, because we thought he would win', Pat says frankly. 'I remember going to the top bar on the new grandstand and having to explain myself to Michael. At this stage we thought we had a handy horse who just hadn't put it all together yet. Going back to the sire, we knew he'd get better over time.' But Pat would not be tempted to use blinkers on the horse for some time.

Then bad luck struck. Happy Clapper was working early one morning in the Randwick dark, before the other horses arrived for trackwork, as is Pat's usual practice, when a fox ran underneath the horse and startled him.

'Foxes come onto the course via the underground tunnel and are a real problem', Pat says. 'The horse bolted on the young Hong Kong apprentice who was riding him that day and bowed a tendon. Vet Chris O'Sullivan suggested we do rehab on the tendon rather than just wrap it in cotton wool before sending him for a long spell. Every morning for a month we iced the tendon, treated the injury with cortisone and then bandaged it.'

O'Sullivan recommended the horse be sent for a six-month spell. Michael Thomas said to give him as much time as he needs, so Pat doubled the horse's time in the paddock. For the best part of a year, Pat kept an eye on Happy Clapper on the family farm.

'Dad always said an injury gives a horse more time to mature. It was a blessing in disguise, because the Clapper came back to racing an entirely different horse. He matured in mind and body, plus he got a lot of love and care up here at Kulnura. He was pretty bloody spoilt, actually. Running free in a paddock was the best thing for him.'

Happy Clapper had almost a full year off and returned to racing as four-year-old maiden in January 2015. 'There was a 1300m race at Kembla Grange I wanted to run him in, so Wayne sent Mitchell Bell's manager a tape of his run down there the previous year. Could we book Mitchell for the race?'

Unfortunately, Bell couldn't commit until his major employer Darley released their nominations for the race, so Pat went to his Plan B. 'Let's just run him at Canterbury and put Blake Shinn on him', he told Michael Thomas.

Happy Clapper lined up a $2.45 favourite in a $50,000 race at Canterbury on Australia Day 2015. The four-year-old broke his maiden, defeating Isorich by a neck. 'Happy Clapper fell in that day. He shouldn't have won. If you watch the replay, when Blake started to improve around the bottom turn at the back of the track, he got into a tussle with Kathy O'Hara on Miello. O'Hara and Shinn were a couple for several years, and she tried to outride him when the competitiveness kicked in.'

It was a great training performance to get the gelding back to racing after a career-threatening bowed tendon and to win first up on the tight Canterbury circuit. More was to follow.

Happy Clapper then won a Benchmark 75 race at Randwick and a Benchmark 80 at Warwick Farm by relatively small margins. 'Like all good horses, Clapper only did what he had to do to win, nothing more. But that was him.' At Randwick, the horse sustained a long run from the back and came five wide to win by a neck. At Warwick Farm, he sat behind the leaders and punched through at the 200m to win by half a length. Blake Shinn was on him in all three victories.

Happy Clapper had another short break before coming back to racing in July 2015. Unfortunately, the horse struck a heavy 9 track at Randwick and was bogged down on the rails, the worse part of the track. 'Blake said all he could do was sit on the horse because his wheels were spinning in the mud.' Happy Clapper was again turned out for a short spell.

Happy Clapper still was a day-to-day proposition even then, Pat says. The injury-plagued galloper resumed '85 per cent fit' at Randwick in October 2015 and did a backflip on his way into the track when the race-day music fired up the crowd. Happy Clapper, with jockey Brenton Avdulla on board, went on to win by a half-length.

Pat gave the strapping five-year-old gelding time to get over that run, easing him up again for five weeks before sending him to another trial, which he won. A 1500m race second up is never ideal, but Happy Clapper had a touch of quality about him. The horse was allocated 60.5kg topweight in a Benchmark 85 at Rosehill Gardens at the end of November.

Happy Clapper's 'sensational win' at Rosehill on November 28, when he made a long-sustained run from well back, turned heads in the Sydney media. Where has this horse been? This unknown gelding lumped 60.5kg off a short break, and ran figures better than any runner in the highly regarded Festival Stakes, run on the same day.

'We knew he would get into the Villiers Stakes with a light weight and that's how Brenton Avdulla ended up on him. Blake couldn't make the 53kgs in the Villiers. We had to win at Rosehill to get a run in the Villiers but, with Michael Thomas' support, we placed the horse very well.'

Happy Clapper took his place in the Group 2 Villiers Stakes (1600m) having won five of his previous six starts. The press saw the Clapper as an exciting new horse on the scene, on the way up. 'It was a tough run before the Villiers so we didn't do much with him since', Pat told an interested press contingent, but he couldn't hold off his enthusiasm after the horse's final gallop before the big race. The horse was ready.

As Pat told son Wayne before the biggest day in the stable's history, 'We've been on this road before with other horses. He's a nice horse, and we've stuck him under the radar as far as weight is concerned, and we've got a good alley … people say enjoy the week. Bullshit!'

Happy Clapper may have been snuck into the race through the back door, but bookies posted him a safe $4.75 favourite. The Villiers had a touch of class about that year including Godolphin import It's Somewhat, already a Group 3 winner in Australia; 2014 Queensland Oaks winner Tinto, Group 3 winning mare Zanbagh, two-time Summer Cup winner I'm Imposing, and Listed Stakes winner Red Excitement also lined up in the race.

Happy Clapper jumped with them and although Brenton Avdulla settled sixth in the back straight, one off the fence and three back from the leader, he somehow got pushed onto the worst part of the track as they entered the straight. As the horses fanned, with It's Somewhat the widest at five horses out, the Clapper's jockey had no option but to go back to the inside on the worse ground of the track, and he drove the horse through to hit the lead at the 100m. Tinto and It's Somewhat finished hard but Happy Clapper had just under a length on them, having overcome track bias to score a memorable win in the Group 2 Villiers Stakes.

'Avdulla up on the inside,' broadcaster Darren Flindell called, 'taking the run that nobody else wanted, and Happy Clapper has burst clear to win the Villiers for Pat Webster'.

Upon dismounting, Avdulla got in first about why he ended up on the worst part of the track. 'I didn't want to be there …' he explained.

Pat shot back, 'I didn't want you there either, but great ride mate'.

'I'll never forget when the horse came back in the enclosure. It was big relief because a lot of people expected him to win. After the race, Racing NSW Steward Marc Van Gestel told me, "Well done Pat, you have a Group 1 horse there, because no other horse did what he was able to do that day".'

Pat had no hesitation in declaring Happy Clapper the best horse he'd trained. 'He has had his injuries … but we have taken our time with him. Happy Clapper is a success story for the little guys.'

'This horse would be pretty scary if he was sound', his jockey chimed in.

If Happy Clapper was 'a blessing', as Pat has often stated, then having son Wayne by his side, and the attendance of numerous grandkids at the track that day, was the icing on the cake. That night the family celebrated the win at their favourite haunt, the Wet Paint restaurant at Bronte, and stories, jokes and jibes bounced back and forth throughout the night.

At the end of 2015, Happy Clapper's record was six wins from just twelve starts culminating in his win in a Randwick mile, Pat's first Group win at the distance. More importantly, the Villiers win earned a ballot exemption for the Group 1 Doncaster Mile (1600m) the following autumn.

The 'Donny'. Pat's dream race.

***

Before Happy Clapper bowed a tendon, his owner Michael Thomas was offered $400,000 for the gelding from Hong Kong interests. The money was a phenomenal return on his original $13,000 investment so the breeder-owner thought long and hard about it, even discussing the offer with his loyal trainer.

'I'm thinking about it,' Pat recalls Michael telling him.

'"If I did sell, you'll get 10 per cent", he told me, which goes to show just the bloke he is.' Thomas turned his back on the deal.

After the gelding's Villiers success, however, a big owner associated with the John Hawkes stable offered Thomas $500,000 for a half share ... but the Clapper would go to Team Hawkes to train. That decision was a much easier to one to make. The answer was a polite no.

Pat has always been thankful that Happy Clapper had only one owner, rather than a syndicate of 'pub trainers' as Pat likes to call them. 'Michael never underestimated the horse but he didn't want to Jonah himself. He wasn't one to make grand statements in the press, like "He'll win today".'

'Horse racing is a fickle business, ruthless even, but Michael backed me and backed his own judgement. The horse went on to win another $6.5 million for him, so it was obviously a great decision!'

CHAPTER 15

Michael's Story

When Michael Thomas' father Jack took on the role of secretary of the ACT Jockey Club in the 1960s, it was largely a family-run operation. 'Basically, it was run from our home', says the owner of Happy Clapper, who was about ten years old at the time and the youngest in the Thomas family. 'There was no other staff other than an honorary treasurer so my parents did everything. Mum would type every word of the race book before sending it to the printer. My brother and I did the barrier draw in school holidays, and all sorts of other jobs such as collecting refunds on the soft drink bottles on track. Once we had collected 50 cents, we would go and have a bet.'

Jack Thomas considered himself to be more of a public servant than a racing fan, but when the two Canberra race clubs amalgamated in the 1960s, he became the inaugural chairman of the Canberra Racing Club, which he held until his death in 1982. Jack may not have had a racing background, but his sons were smitten with the sport. 'We had a booming little business selling the race books,' says Michael, 'but the real money was buying lead pencils from Coles and cutting them up, sharpening them and selling them with the race books'.

As a teenager, Michael worked for the on-course tote in various capacities, running around and getting the official finishing numbers from the judges, and becoming a TAB operator when he was a uni student. 'I then became a bookie's clerk', he says. 'That was enjoyable, but my older brother got itchy feet and later became a bookmaker.'

As a punter, Michael struck gold winning the trifecta on the 1981 Melbourne Cup – Just a Dash, El Laurena and Flashing Light – winning $39,000, 'which was a lot of money for someone who had very little of it at the time. I thought I would just take a semester off from my accountancy degree because the money was burning a hole in my pocket, and I never went back. I punted successfully for a while, and with the windfall I had the funds to launch our bookmaking careers.'

The Thomas brothers then started buying and breeding horses.

'Paul and I got involved with a couple of horses with Keith Dryden as trainer, who put us onto a mare called Vale Nymph', he says. The daughter of Avon Valley was no star on the track and the best of her five progeny to win a race was her first foal, the stakes-placed Green Waters, son of Opera Prince.

'Green Waters was a good country performer, winning fifteen races. They were cavalier days,' Michael recalls, 'and we won a lot of money backing it'.

The second foal Vale Nymph produced was Winifred's Prayer, a daughter of 1991 Golden Slipper winner Tierce. Winifred's Prayer had one start at Canberra for a win, but never raced again. Of the six foals she produced, the five to reach the track were all above average. Busking, daughter of Encosta de Lago, was Winifred's Prayer's second foal. Her half-brother Gunfire Messiah won eleven races while Thankgodyou'rehere, son of Secret Savings, was Winifred's Prayer's final foal and perhaps the best of the bunch.

'I sent Winifred's Prayer to Encosta De Lago in 1998, when the stallion was just starting out. The fee at the time was $7700 – Encosta De Lago later stood for $220,000, so I thought that was a really good placement.' Winifred's Prayer missed in 1998 so Thomas sent the mare back to Encosta De Lago the following year and produced Busking in 2000.

But breeding and racing horses is an expensive business and Michael Thomas was advised to sell some of his stock. 'Encosta De Lago was the flavour of the month, and seeing I had bred Busking for a bargain, I felt I had to cash in.'

Busking was sold to trainer John Morrisey for $40,000, but Thomas regretted the move pretty much straight away. 'It was the first time I had sold a member of Winifred's Prayer's family, and I didn't really want to part with Busking because I felt there was a brilliant streak in the family … and she could be the broodmare that continued the line. Funny enough, John Morrisey bought the horse because he remembered the mother working trackwork at Canberra. She ran like the wind.'

Busking only won one of her sixteen starts, but was a regular placegetter and posted a good fourth in the Ken Russel Memorial Classic. By the time she finished her racing career 'Encosta' broodmares had become very popular, and Busking was snapped up by Woodlands Stud in the Hunter Valley. Darley, Sheikh Mohammed bin Rashid Al Maktoum's global thoroughbred stallion operation, acquired Woodlands in 2008.

When Darley decided to sell her in 2010, Busking had produced four foals. Santana, which raced as White Coffee in Singapore and won eleven races, and Gig, which was later Group placed on three occasions. 'In foal to Irish Derby winner Teofilo, Busking turned up at the Melbourne March thoroughbred sale', Michael remembers. 'I had been a client of Darley's and, after talking to them, they assured me the mare was in good order and I brought her at auction for $13,000. They had systems in place – it was all about stock control – but they did not want to sell her too cheaply because it would negate the service fee for Teofilo.'

Almost a full decade after breeding Busking, the mare was back with Thomas. 'I lost her, regretted losing her, and got her back.' And she had the good manners, he says, to have Happy Clapper inside her.

The name of the Teofilo-Busking progeny came about over a discussion with a couple of friends and an equal number of bottles of red wine consumed in Washington DC. 'Winifred's Prayer was the mother of Busking and that has a slightly religious undertone', Michael explains. 'Teofilo is Greek for "beloved of God" but the progeny is named after the Cuban Olympic boxer Teofilo Stephenson, so I went for the more religious name.'

In the 1970s, churches were full of people playing guitars, singing and dancing down the aisles – 'enthusiastic religious congregations,' as Thomas remembers it – and popularly known as 'happy clappies'. Happy Clapper sounded better.

'A horse called Happy Trails had a bit of a cult following at the time, so I had a theory that putting the word "Happy" in the name would bring us good luck. If you get a good name like Happy Clapper and the horse is any good, supporters are rusted on for life.'

It is now history that Happy Clapper went to Randwick trainer Pat Webster as compensation for losing Thankgodyou'rehere. The Clapper was a big gelding that needed a lot of patience, and Thomas was in no hurry to rush him to the track. 'I had the hots for him more than Pat. I was very impressed with his barrier trials but Pat wanted more time with him and I never stopped him … as the old racing adage goes, "there's always hope until they race".'

Happy Clapper had his first run at Kembla Grange in July 2013. 'Pat said the horse wasn't ready and the race was just going to be a step in his education. I told him he might be surprised. The horse ran third and probably should have won.'

The gelding's placing in a Group 3 race at his fourth start confirmed his potential at an early stage, Thomas says. 'He was then spelled and resumed in a midweeker at Kensington and was beaten. Forget he went around, the jockey assured us.'

A fox then ran under him at trackwork one morning. The horse took fright, and after taking his trackwork rider on a scenic tour of the Randwick circuit, did a tendon.

Michael believes this was a blessing in disguise. 'We followed the vet's advice to the letter and didn't race him for a year. During the enforced layoff, he grew into his big body at his own pace.'

Happy Clapper was a still a maiden when he returned to racing as a four-year-old but won three consecutive races before failing on a bog track.

Was he still a group horse in the making? 'Pat always said to me, "one step at a time", but it cost me nothing just to hope, although to be honest I was thinking he was a good Saturday horse in the making.'

Happy Clapper came back as a lightly-raced five-year-old and won two races before his victory in the Group 2 Villiers Stakes. 'Looking back, the win was well-planned and well-executed by Pat.' Happy Clapper was thrown in at the weights and won by a length as a $4.80 favourite.

For Michael, the real eye-opener as far as the horse's ability was concerned was when he ran second in the 2016 Doncaster Mile (1600m) and then graduated to WFA class. 'In those days, no horse went from a Villiers to the Doncaster. We had 50.5kg in the Doncaster, got beaten by Winx, who was just starting out on her journey, and then backed up seven days later in the Queen Elizabeth Stakes and ran third. We realised then he was a serious horse.'

Happy Clapper had a hoof problem in 2016 but was only beaten by half a length in running fourth in the 2016 Epsom. 'He never came right that prep. We went off to the Cox Plate ... its Melbourne, it's the Cox Plate and it's Winx: everything you don't want when your horse isn't firing.'

When Happy Clapper was beaten by It's Somewhat on a heavy 8 track in the 2017 Doncaster, Michael Thomas walked off the Randwick track thinking, 'well that's our hope to win a Group 1. Maybe we're destined never to win one'.

Instead, Happy Clapper went to another level.

The following spring, the seven-year-old gelding came out and won the Group 2 Tramway (1400m), the Group 1 Epsom (1600m) and then finished unlucky seconds in two more races – the Group 1 Craven Plate (2000m) and the Emirates Stakes (2000m) at Flemington. The following autumn he won two more Group 1s, the Canterbury Stakes (1300m) and the Doncaster Mile (1600m), both at Randwick.

'We really had our heads around what we needed to do with the horse so why not run him in a Group 1 first up over 1300m? Things seem to click into place more easily at Randwick where he doesn't have to travel.'

'Then he won his Doncaster!' Michael says. 'It was all a bit too much to take in.'

Michael didn't realise Pat hadn't trained a Group 1 winner before because he knew he had won the TJ Smith Stakes twice, and that is now a Group 1 race. 'Only, it wasn't back then. When a journo told me the Epsom was Pat's first Group 1, I couldn't believe it. "What?" But I was delighted for him. Pat's been waiting all his training life to get a Group 1 horse and I'm glad it's my horse that gave him that.'

What was the feeling like to finally win a Group 1 as an owner? 'It's relief, the monkey's off my back. So much excitement compressed into a small period of time, and all of a sudden, its released.' Not that Michael is overly emotional. 'It makes me laugh when people get excited and emotional on a racetrack … what is it that makes people act so differently to their everyday life? I ended up just like the rest of them when The Clapper won the Doncaster. It was exhilarating!'

Michael was happy to remain in the background while the press focused on the horse and its laconic trainer. 'I like to watch the race quietly in the grandstand and away from the cameras in the enclosure. It's more exciting than watching the race at ground level on the big screen. If I wanted to watch the screen, I could do that at home on the couch! The cameras can't find me and the media don't even know what I look like.'

'Pat's the racing writer's and Sky Channel's choice, the "go to" man for a quote or a good story. I'm happy with that. I don't need to be asked how I feel after a big win.'

Owner and trainer have a great relationship. 'I have full control of Clapper because I'm the sole owner, but then I don't get control because Pat's the trainer', he laughs. 'Pat and I always discuss everything regarding Clapper. He likes to thinks out loud, "well what do you think about such and such?" and I say to him "Why do you ask? The trainer always gets his way".'

"It's something I've always said to him. "Pat, I'm not a horse trainer", and I've never changed his mind yet!'

They've never had a disagreement either. 'It made me feel good that he was spending every waking and working moment on the horse. That has been critical to the success.'

On the same day Happy Clapper claimed the $500,000 Group 1 Canterbury Stakes, the gelding's half-brother Not A Single Cent won the Group 2 VRC Sire's Produce Stakes (1400m) at Flemington, giving Michael Thomas a double celebration. After being purchased by Ciaron Maher Racing for $280,000 at the Magic Millions Gold Coast Yearling sale, Thomas brought back a 25 per cent share in the colt as 'insurance', he says.

First prize in 2018 Doncaster Mile was a massive $1,740,000. Thomas didn't mind collecting the trophies either. 'I'd been eyeing off some of the championship trophies through my binoculars … diamond encrusted horseheads, I wouldn't mind one of those.

'There are actually two owner's trophies for the Doncaster – the second is a replica of the perpetual trophy that the AJC had in place decades before. It's a handsome silver trophy, with as lid that needs to be unsoldered when it gets used as an urn for my ashes when I die!' he laughs.

But the Clapper team didn't get ahead of themselves. It's all been about the horse and they've gone about their business very humbly. But when Happy Clapper suffered his bleeding attack in Melbourne in 2018, the real fear was that the horse wouldn't come back from it. 'I walked off the course thinking that's it, we've had a great run.' But the horse came back.

Happy Clapper ran second to Winx in the Apollo Stakes (1400m) and then made the champion mare earn her victory in the Chipping Norton (1600m). 'I knew Winx would win but I think people were happy that we made a race of it. Some were critical that we may have overtaxed him, but I believe that run was well within his capabilities.'

Thomas is hopeful the horse will race on as a nine-year-old. 'The Clapper is a Randwick horse ... I would like him to get through the spring in form ready for the autumn. We'll aim for lighter campaigns and not be tempted by Melbourne anymore. Let's enjoy the rest of the ride and the horse will let us know when he's had enough.'

There have been many restless nights during the horse's racing preparation – 'even my friends say I am a different person when Happy Clapper is racing', Michael admits, so he can understand the decision to retire Winx. 'Chris Waller has a big stable to look after and has devoted a lot of time and energy to Winx. He's now relieved of that burden and they retired her at the peak of her powers. I am sure there was a huge sigh of relief because they successfully transitioned her to the next stage of her career without any mishaps or sense of disappointment.'

Michael has had a lot of people say to him, wouldn't it be good if there wasn't a Winx? 'There are more "what ifs" than just Winx', he admits. 'What if I couldn't have been bothered buying Busking back? That was a 50/50 call. What if I had decided to sell the progeny rather than race it? That's what breeders normally do. What if I hadn't have sent it to Pat Webster? Would the horse have been as successful without Pat's patience and hands-on approach? What if the Clapper hadn't made it back to the track after the fox ran under him? What if the fox didn't run under him? That sent him on a completely different path.'

There are just so many other 'ifs' to consider.

'I think about it in these terms ... at the end of the day, I have a world-class horse which has won $6.8 million in prizemoney. I would have to be pretty miserable as a person to be looking at the "what ifs". I hit the biggest jackpot of all time.'

Happy Clapper hasn't changed his life. 'Journos like to count the difference in prizemoney Clapper could have won with Winx out of the way but I'm not the least worried about that. I am not the world's greatest consumer; my car is ten years old and I live in a modest home. I've had money before and been a successful bookmaker and punter.

'Put it this way, the money is not a life-changer but having the horse take us to heights I never imagined is.'

Michael Thomas owns the last of Busking's progeny, also by Not a Single Doubt, named One Man Band. 'He's an unraced rising three-year-old with Matt Dale', he says. 'My non-racing friends ask me if I might get another good horse. I tell them there's only one Happy Clapper in many, many lifetimes. Not everyone gets that.

'I'm not looking for the next Happy Clapper because there won't be one.'

CHAPTER 16

Group 1 Glory

Pat Webster has met many interesting and high-profile people in his life. It says a lot about what sort of person he is. Prime ministers, rock stars, millionaires, battlers ... he's mixed with them all and treats everyone the same. As he finds them.

Even though he wasn't a Group 1-winning trainer with the profile of Gai Waterhouse or Chris Waller, he had carved a niche for himself in the sport. When he and Chrissy were in Hong Kong some time back, enjoying dinner in a crowded Chinese restaurant, an Australian businessman popped his head around the corner and said, 'Pat Webster!'

Pat had never met the man before, and asked him how he had recognised him. 'Easy', the stranger said. 'You're the only other white bloke in here.'

Happy Clapper was set an ambitious autumn program in 2017, the gelding running in two Group 1 Weight For Age (WFA) races – the Canterbury Stakes (1300m) and the George Ryder Stakes (1500m) – before taking on the handicappers in the Doncaster Mile (1600m), for which he had been allocated a lightweight 50.5kg. No horse had won the Villiers-Doncaster double since Wedding Day, almost a century before in the 1916-17, but the Clapper team were hopeful.

'I asked Melbourne trainer Robbie Laing what makes a good WFA horse? "Having a big bastard like Happy Clapper helps", he told me. The Clapper is a magnificent beast, but he'd only been a handicapper up until then. Some horses make the WFA grade, some don't. We just didn't know until we tried.'

And then they bumped into a budding champion named Winx.

Having won the Sunshine Coast Guineas-Queensland Oaks double at the end of her three-year-old season, Winx had returned to racing the previous spring to win the Group 2 Theo Marks Stakes (1400m), the Group 1 Epsom Handicap (1600m) and Group 1 WS Cox Plate (2040m) in successive starts. In the autumn, the mare extended her winning streak to nine wins, culminating with a win in the 2016 Doncaster.

'The real fear was we might not get our Group 1 now because Winx was just too good.' Not that it would stop him from taking her on.

Winx beat Happy Clapper quite easily in the George Ryder, but with a massive 8.5kg switch in the weights, could the five-year-old gelding turn the tables on the mare in the Doncaster?

'She wasn't the Winx she is now. But she gave us 6.5kg in the Doncaster and still beat us two lengths.' The Clapper came from well back under hard riding from Brenton Avdulla and made his challenge just as Winx got a split in the middle of the pack. But Hugh Bowman had ridden the mare for luck, rather than sweeping down the outside in her usual fashion, and the move paid off.

Even after coming so close to winning his dream race, Pat could see the silver lining. 'If Happy Clapper had won that Doncaster, the horse would have been weighted out of the Epsom he ultimately won.'

Happy Clapper then ran third in the Group 1 Queen Elizabeth II Stakes (2000m) behind Luca Valentina and The United States, which was a phenomenal leap in class from the handicaps he had been competing in at the start of his five-year-old season. The gelding had a short letup – he rested at Kulnura for just ten days – and then went straight back into training.

Happy Clapper opened his spring campaign with a moderate fifth in the Group 2 Tramway Stakes (1400m) on a heavy 8 track at Randwick. The gelding was uncomfortable in the ground behind the Godolphin miler Hauraki, and beaten by about four and a half lengths. He was considered unlucky in the Group 3 Bill Ritchie Handicap (1400m) a fortnight later, finishing sixth without getting a clear run at the leaders, but subsequent events proved the horse was not at his best.

Pat remembers that time well. 'On my way to the track, about 2.30 in the morning, Wayne rang me and said, "Dad, don't panic because we don't know what's happening yet". That's when I started to panic!'

There was heat in one of Happy Clapper's legs. 'In the stable yard, he must have rolled and ran a piece of metal into the back of his hoof ... an old, rusted bit of "reo". We x-rayed him straight away.'

Vet Chris O'Sullivan stuck a needle into the area of the hoof that had been penetrated and said, "You might be blessed, Pat. If you were going to have that injury that's the best place to have it".

The vet then suggested they put the horse on a course of penicillin. '"We can't do that", I said. "He's in the Epsom Handicap in two weeks' time".'

The vet's response was sobering. 'Let's worry about saving the horse's life first ... if his hoof becomes infected, he could die.'

For the next ten days, Happy Clapper had two shots of penicillin a day, finishing the course just before the big race on 1 October 2016. 'The penicillin flattened the horse, no doubt', Pat says. 'He didn't come right in the coat. I was concerned.'

Pat was looking for an edge, something to spark the horse on the day of the race, and suggested to wife Chrissy that he might experiment by putting blinkers on the horse. 'Chrissy said don't change things now. I was only second guessing myself, of course, but given what I know now, it might have made a big difference.'

Pat's mood brightened when Happy Clapper drew barrier one. Brenton Avdulla could sit behind the leaders and make his run at the top of the straight. 'Happy Clapper came out and ran fourth, beaten under a length. What a mighty effort! It was his worst placing ever in a Randwick mile, and he wasn't quite himself that day.'

The Gai Waterhouse-trained Fabrizzio led by eight lengths in the back straight, with Happy Clapper running fourth on the fence. Fabrizzio still led by six lengths when the field straightened, but the Clapper was momentarily held up. When he saw daylight, Happy Clapper was flat, one-paced.

Fabrizzio was swamped at the 100m, with Le Romain, Macintosh and Dibayani hitting the lead and Happy Clapper a length behind them. Right on the line, Hauraki launched at Dibayani and MacIntosh with the Clapper half a length away in fourth. Hauraki had come from last to win, but it was a mighty effort by the Clapper.

Although the horse still wasn't his old self, the team persevered with Melbourne. Winx was looking for a second straight win in the WS Cox Plate, while the Clapper was having his first look at the Melbourne way of going on the testing Mooney Valley track.

Everything was against the horse in Melbourne … Australia's toughest WFA race, running the opposite way for the first time, and taking on Winx again when the gelding was not at his best. 'Fuck me, how are we going to beat her', was Pat's blunt assessment.

Happy Clapper finished sixth in Cox Plate, beaten by some eleven lengths. Winx won by a record eight lengths but the Clapper picked up $100,000 for his connections. The gelding's first campaign in Melbourne finished with a listless ninth in the Group 1 LKS Mackinnon Stakes (2000m) on Derby Day.

It was also Brenton Avdulla's last ride on the gelding. Avdulla wasn't available for the six-year-old's return in 2017 in Canberra's National Sprint (1400m), leaving the door for Blake Shinn to take the ride and form the perfect partnership with the budding champion.

'We took Happy Clapper to Canberra because Michael Thomas lives there and it suited the horse to start his campaign over that distance', Pat says. The Clapper carried the maximum topweight of 60.5kg but when the field jumped, his back legs were crossed and he stumbled out last.

'That could have been a career ending run right there', Pat admits. Happy Clapper was last coming into the straight and it was an amazing run to finish second, beaten under two lengths by Gold Symphony.

'Many people think I sacked Brenton, but that wasn't the case', Pat says. 'When the Clapper came back in the autumn, Brenton wouldn't commit to the Doncaster ride because he thought he was riding one of Chris Waller's. I wanted the same jockey to ride the Clapper at Newcastle and in the Doncaster, so we had to make the decision then and there.'

Pat and Michael Thomas chose Blake Shinn.

'I know Brenton was disappointed, but that's racing. The Clapper gave him his first Group win in the Villiers, and he'd run second on him in two Doncaster Miles.' The only regret Pat has is that Avdulla never rode Happy Clapper when the gelding was wearing blinkers. 'The Clapper was a different horse with blinkers on ... lengths better.'

The problem remained that Blake Shinn couldn't make the 54.5kg weight the horse was allotted for the Doncaster. 'Blake needed at least another kilo, so we ran the Clapper in the Newmarket Stakes in Newcastle (1400m) so he would incur a small penalty.' Pat even rang the Racing NSW handicapper to ensure the gelding would be rehandicapped if he won in Newcastle.

Blake Shinn rode Happy Clapper to an easy three-and-a-half-length win in the Newmarket and recommitted to the Doncaster Mile, in which he was reallocated 55.5kg. All was going to plan. Then Randwick delivered a heavy 8 track on Doncaster day.

'The Clapper was fourth, back on the fence, and you could see when he straightened that he wasn't comfortable in the going', Pat says. Shinn brought the horse into the middle of the track, but It's Somewhat led all the way, hanging on for a half-length win. 'At the 200m, I still thought he'd get to the leader but it didn't happen.'

Running in the Group 1 Queen Elizabeth II Stakes (2000m) was an afterthought, but the prospect of taking on Winx once more was tempered by the fact that the race was at Randwick and, always the pragmatist, Pat says, 'the minor prizemoney was pretty bloody good'. The Clapper finished fifth on a soft 7 track, beaten by almost 8 lengths.

***

In 2011, former star Sydney apprentice Josh Adams received a seven month suspension after testing positive to having a banned substance in his system. Adams' admission that he was 'guilty of stupidity more than anything' glossed over the bigger issues he was dealing with.

'He was hanging around people he didn't normally associate with, but a random drug test at Gosford the day after the Golden Slipper changed all that.' Adams put it down to 'an honest accident' and entered an early guilty plea.

Pat was already a Racing NSW counsellor and said at the time, 'Josh has volunteered to be a role model in future, so they can learn from his mistakes'. But first Josh had to learn from his mistakes.

Some months later, Webster bumped into Adams at a Bunnings store on the Central Coast – the former top apprentice was a long way from his best. Suspended after his drugs bust, he was overweight, his skin was blotchy and he was obviously under the influence of drugs. Pat spoke to him about what he was doing to his life and invited him to the family farm and started guiding the young hoop on his comeback.

Adams returned to racing after serving his suspension, riding Pat's horses in trackwork. He was still 'a work in progress' when Happy Clapper returned to training, but with Blake Shinn riding in Melbourne when the Clapper returned in the Group 2 Tramway Stakes (1400m), Pat talked to Michael

Thomas about giving Adams the ride.

'Michael agreed with my judgment', Pat says.

Josh Adams rode the perfect race on Clapper in the Tramway, defeating Tom Melbourne by a little under a length. 'When Josh won on Happy Clapper I cried because it was like winning ten Group 1s – it meant so much', Pat told journalist Andrew Webster. The next day, Adams was banned for three months after dropping his hands on a favourite at Moree and getting beaten. The hoop was back to square one in his comeback.

After winning the Tramway, Happy Clapper was at the mercy of the handicapper when weights were released for the Group 1 Epsom. When the gelding was allotted 56.5kg, Pat joked in the press, 'He didn't win that well', but it was an argument he knew he couldn't win.

Happy Clapper readied for the Epsom with a run in the Group 1 George Main Stakes (1600m) and another showdown with Winx. On her way to winning a third straight WS Cox Plate, the 'Super Mare' defeated runaway leader Red Excitement in the Chelmsford Stakes (1600m) in a brilliant performance.

Winx had become *Winx*.

In the George Main, Happy Clapper jumped well, settled midfield and travelled kindly in the run. 'At the half mile I felt like the winner', Blake Shinn said after the race, but after hitting the lead at the 200m, rival jockey Hugh Bowman gave Winx a crack with the whip and the race was all over. The Clapper still beat the others by four and a half lengths but, for once, Pat was almost lost for words after watching Winx in action.

'Our horse ran the race of his life but he's run into a freak.'

Winx's continued success at WFA meant that she was now weighted out of the major handicap races, leaving the way free for Happy Clapper to claim a Group 1. In the 2017 Epsom, Happy Clapper was allotted 56.5kg but when original topweight Black Heart Bart, and then Humidor, Le Romain and Vega Magic were each scratched, weights were raised 0.5kg to ensure the mandatory 57kg topweight.

Happy Clapper wore the Number 1 saddlecloth in the Epsom carrying 57kg, the same weight Flagrante carried in 1996 when that horse won the race in record time. Second favourite Egg Tart was scratched on the eve of the race, but Happy Clapper now had to also carry the weight of public expectations as a $2.70 favourite.

'The Clapper has a habit of having a bite of the rail or throwing out a kick when we take him to the races, but the horse was just so quiet on Epsom day. He was flat, which really worried us'.

Pat likes to watch the Clapper on race day on a small TV near the enclosure. 'I had a horse in a big race once, and when it was leading by four and five lengths my vet tapped me on the shoulder and said, "Well you've won this" … and by the time I turned back around it got beat.

'I like to be by myself when I watch the race because I put a lot of pressure on myself. I didn't sleep much leading into the Epsom I was so worried Winx had flattened him in the George Main. Everyone was expecting him to win, which was hard. I'd never won a Group 1 before and were in a fucking Epsom as a $2.70 favourite.'

At the jump, Blake Shinn parked the Clapper behind leader Red Excitement and gave the gelding a dream run. 'The speed was hot, but he always travelled well', the hoop said after the race. Hitting the lead at the 300m, Shinn later reflected, 'Maybe he got there a little bit early for my liking – he was a sitting shot'.

When that big-race deceiver Tom Melbourne ranged up to Happy Clapper, Pat thought to himself, 'Well, if we don't beat him, we're in a bit of trouble'. Form analyst Ron Dufficy had given 'Old Tom' an almighty spray before the race, declaring him a 'non-winner'. The former Melbourne gelding was now trained by Chris Waller – Winx's trainer – who squeezed the best run of Tom Melbourne's career out of him, but the Clapper was better still.

Happy Clapper responded under Blake Shinn's riding to win by a half-length, breaking Flagrante's track record. 'There won't be a more popular Epsom victory than Happy Clapper's here today', Sky Channel's Greg

Radley said after the horses crossed the line. 'A very popular horse, and a very, very likeable trainer in Pat Webster.'

Pat had waited fifty years for his first Group 1 success and it was well worth it. It was only fitting that it was at Royal Randwick too, where he had been apprenticed as a teenage jockey and trained for almost forty years.

'I thought he was too close,' Pat later reflected, 'but the Clapper was too good'. Pat's first thought after the win was for suspended jockey Josh Adams. Pat got on the phone to him straight after the race. 'I just wanted to check that he was okay.'

After fifteen winners at Group 2 and 3 level, Pat Webster had done it. 'Not quite a Doncaster', Pat remarked, but that too would come soon. It was just Happy Clapper's 28th race start, and the win was a masterclass of patience by trainer and owner. Finally, the pressure he put on himself was released.

'I wouldn't have had more than a dozen runners in Group 1s over the years but the most important thing I received after the Epsom win was the respect of my peers. Until you win a Group 1, it's hard to get that respect … especially at Randwick. There's a different body language – a swagger even – about trainers who have won Group 1s, so I can't say not winning one didn't matter to me … it did', he says. 'I just never thought it would happen to me with such a small string.'

Happy Clapper almost won another Group 1 at his next start. Sent out a short $1.50 favourite in the Craven Plate (2000m) at Randwick, the gelding got too far back and his run ended just before the line, giving victory to the $23 shot Classic Uniform by a long head. 'It's hard to be critical of the horse when he's given us so much joy', Pat says, the loss still hurting. 'But the truth is, he's had several goes at 2000m without being able to win. His best distance is a mile.'

Pat pushed on with a Melbourne campaign, targeting the WS Cox Plate for a second successive year. 'The cold hard fact is that the country's best WFA race is run in Melbourne, so you have no option but to go there. The

Clapper did it twice, and raced against Winx at her peak, although he was never really comfortable on the track.'

Ridden by premier Melbourne jockey Damien Oliver after regular rider Blake Shinn had a prior engagement on the import Humidor, Happy Clapper got shuffled back to last in the Cox Plate and finished sixth. Winx won a record-equalling third WS Cox Plate by a half-length from Humidor, with Happy Clapper finishing sixth, six lengths behind them.

'Damien Oliver said that if he didn't have a bumping dual early in the race, he would definitely have run second.' Oliver later was suspended for twenty meetings for causing interference to Royal Symphony and missed the entire Spring Carnival. Stewards alleged that after 100m of the race, Oliver was working across from his outside barrier (9) and pushed inward onto Royal Symphony, which was ridden by Dean Yendall. The stewards reported that Happy Clapper made 'heavy contact' with Royal Symphony and applied 'unnecessary pressure' on the other horse, forcing him to shift in.

Oliver defended his actions, saying that the only option was to sit four and five horses wide and that he thought Yendall was heading for the fence. Happy Clapper made a wide charge at the leaders on the turn, but the early buffeting told in the straight. The $100,000 prizemoney for sixth place was ample compensation for the team.

In 2017, the Group 1 Emirates Stakes (2000m), formally the Mackinnon Stakes, was run on the Saturday *after* the Melbourne Cup for the first time. Happy Clapper had not been set for the race and was never going to run, but the gelding took no ill effects from the Cox Plate and was jumping out of his skin. Happy Clapper started at an $8 chance behind the imports Folkswood ($3.60), Gingernuts ($6), Tosen Stardom ($6.50) and Gailo Chop (also $8), and carried the No.1 saddlecloth in the classic.

'I was standing in the trainer's room watching on TV when Gingernuts was scratched at the barrier. As the field passed the 600m, a ginger-haired bloke standing next to me started having a heart attack, slid down the wall and lay flat on his back. The horses were at the turn when I grabbed him and turned him over, putting him on his side and clearing his airway. I put some water on his face as the field hit the line. When Melbourne trainer Robert Smerdon walked past, I asked him how the Clapper went.'

Happy Clapper finished second, beaten by the Darren Weir trained Tosen Stardom. Pat missed the finish of the Group 1 race, ensuring the stranger sprawled out on the ground was okay, but he was proud of his horse's effort.

'And I never heard from the guy again, not even a thank you card!'

CHAPTER 17

Third Time's A Charm

In the early 1990s, a young New Zealand strapper named Chris Waller came to Sydney with Paddy Busuttin, the trainer of the champion Cups horse Castletown. 'Chris always says I was the second Australian he ever met', Pat Webster says. 'He has always had beautiful manners and respect, which is saying a lot for a Kiwi. He still calls me Mr Webster. We had him and Paddy over for dinner when they were staying at my stables at Randwick, and Chris can still remember what Chrissy cooked for dinner.'

When Waller started out as a trainer in Australia in 2000, forging a career that would garner multiple metropolitan training premierships, Chrissy Webster's mother wrote a reference for him to the Sydney Turf Club to secure stables at Rosehill.

Back in the autumn of 1991, however, Castletown was being prepared for the major staying races in Sydney. Having run second to Just a Dancer in the AJC Sydney Cup (3200m), both horses backed up in the AJC St Leger. In the week before the race, Pat received a phone call from the anxious strapper, Chris Waller. Paddy Busuttin was under the weather and Castletown needed a track gallop before the big race on Saturday.

'Mr Webster, Paddy is not feeling well and I have to gallop Castletown this morning. What do I do?'

'Do you remember what Paddy did with the horse before he won the Wellington Cup?' Pat asked Waller. 'Then go and do that again …'

'And he did!' Pat laughs. Castletown turned the tables on Just A Dancer in the St Leger.

Almost thirty years later, Waller is the premier Sydney trainer with more than 100 Group 1 wins to his credit, as well as being the man who guided the great Winx to a world record thirty-three wins in succession.

'Some people knock Chris because of the enormous success he's had but they don't see where he's come from', Pat says. 'I did.'

In the first three months of 2018, Waller trained the best horse in the world … well, on grass at least. Heading the Longines World's Best Racehorse Rankings, Gun Runner (USA) tied with Winx with a rating of 129. With Gun Runner winning on dirt tracks, Winx stood alone as the world's turf champion. West Coast (USA) was third, on 124 points, but Happy Clapper was fourth, tied with Great Britain import Redkirk Warrior, on 121.

Pat Webster would continue his friendship with Waller, and his training rivalry, into the Winx-Happy Clapper era. 'Chris is a little wary of me because of what I know', Pat laughs. 'If the journos interview me before a big race, Chris Waller always asks them, "What has he been telling you now?"'

For the third year in succession, Pat targeted the Doncaster Mile with Happy Clapper in 2018. With Winx focusing solely on a WFA program, the 'Donny' was there to win if the Clapper was good enough. No doubt the gelding would come up against Winx in the lead up to the Doncaster, and the champion mare would again provide the benchmark for how well Pat's star was going this preparation.

Happy Clapper was set for a first up kill in the Group 1 Canterbury Stakes (1300m). Originally run at Canterbury, as the name suggests, the race was transferred to Randwick in 2014. Although a lesser light in the cannon of Group 1s on the racing calendar, Pat says, 'it was still a Group 1 race and they're bloody hard to win!'

Pat only wished the race was over 1400m, fearing the gelding's rivals may have an edge over the shorter course, but he didn't want to jinx Happy Clapper's chances by doubting its ability now. The gelding was absolutely flying in training.

Blake Shinn returned from suspension to resume his partnership with Happy Clapper in the Bisley Workwear Canterbury Stakes. Punters backed the horses from $6.00 into a $4.60 favourite, in an open race, after the Clapper again drew well in barrier 1. Gai Waterhouse's Group 1-winning mare Global Glamour led into the straight but the Clapper, three back on the inside, bullocked his way to the centre of the track and finished over the top of them to win by just over a length.

'Happy Clapper got checked badly at the 400m but still won', Pat says proudly. 'It wasn't as good as winning an Epsom or a Doncaster, but it proved the Clapper's Group 1 success in the Epsom was no fluke.'

After the Clapper's victory, Pat was invited to drinks with the race sponsor and members of the ATC committee. 'I remember the Bisley shirts guy was standing there with his wife, so I told him I liked his shirts and wore them on the farm but I didn't like the double pockets. This put him on the back foot so I went in again. "And how about you put a bit more prizemoney into the kick?" I kidded him. "$290,000 is a bit light on for a Group 1."'

Australia Turf Club Vice-Chair Julia Ritchie reminded Pat that it might not be the right time to bring up the issue. 'But I didn't care', Pat laughs. 'I just said what I wanted to because I was on such a high.'

Happy Clapper was allocated 57kg for the Doncaster – the same weight he carried to victory in the previous year's Epsom after weights were raised – but Pat was having difficulty in getting Blake Shinn's manager to commit to the Doncaster ride. 'Blake was promised the ride on Humidor, whom he had run second to Winx in the Cox Plate, and his manager was playing ducks and drakes with me.'

'I wanted Blake,' says Pat, 'because he had the confidence in the horse to get the job done'.

The veteran trainer rang premier Melbourne jockey Damien Oliver directly, bypassing Olly's racing manager. 'Could you ride Clapper in the George Ryder and Doncaster?' Pat asked him.

'"Pat, I'd love to", Olly said, so I rang Ray Thomas at the *Daily Telegraph* and told him as much. Damien Oliver has agreed to ride Happy Clapper.'

Pat ran into Shinn's manager at Gosford races and gave him an almighty spray. 'I have a good jockey committed to both races', he told the manager. 'After the races on Saturday, that's the end of it. If Blake doesn't give me an answer, I'll use Olly.'

'The manager was going to pieces in front of me, but I just wanted Blake to commit', Pat says. '"Mate," I told him, "you'll end up with shingles at this rate". The manager rang back that night and said Blake would ride Clapper both races. As a trainer you have to play hardball with jockeys sometimes, even the top ones.'

Happy Clapper's next start loomed as another showdown with Winx in the Group 1 George Ryder Stakes (1500m) on Golden Slipper Day. When the rankings of the world's Top 100 races were released at the start of 2018, the George Ryder (equal 9th in the world) was rated the third best Australian race behind only the Queen Elizabeth II Stakes (second after the Arche de Triumph) and the WS Cox Plate (eq 7th). No doubt Winx's dominance of all three races since 2015 pushed them up the world list, but Happy Clapper also took his place in those races, often running second to the great mare.

Winx started her preparation with a soft win in the Group 1 Chipping Norton Stakes (1600m), the mare's 23rd successive victory. Regular rider Hugh Bowman had been suspended earlier that year, and rather than run Winx in the Apollo Stakes (1400m) with another jockey, Chris Waller scratched the mare and sent her to the barrier trails instead.

Racing second up, Winx had to come back 100m in the George Ryder. She was vulnerable. 'I speak to Chris Waller on a regular basis and he later admitted that going to that race he was concerned the horse might get beat', Pat says. 'I never had the Clapper going so good.'

This was their chance. 'If we were ever going to beat Winx this was it. I was quietly confident, but then it had to rain.'

Rosehill produced a soft 7 track on Golden Slipper Day, far from ideal for Happy Clapper. 'I said to Blake, naturally it's a Group 1 and if we can beat her then beat her, but I don't want you pulling the whip and flattening him. We still wanted some horse left for the Doncaster … that was his grand final.'

A select field of just six runners took their place in the George Ryder. Happy Clapper raced behind the leader, Invincible Gem, with Winx settling down at the back of the field. The Clapper challenged on the turn as Invincible Gem quickened the speed, but in a lightning move, Bowman brought Winx into the race three wide. The Godolphin colt Kementari tried to go with them, but Happy Clapper and Winx moved clear to fight out the finish.

For a moment, the Clapper went with Winx, stride for stride, but the mare had the momentum and pushed to line, beat Happy Clapper by three-quarters of a length, with Kementari another length away in third.

'Stewards later questioned Blake Shinn for not using enough vigour but we were only trying to protect the horse', says Pat. 'Winx was too good … again.'

Two weeks later, Happy Clapper took his place in the $3,000,000 Doncaster Mile carrying the No.3 saddlecloth behind Humidor (58kg) and Tosen Stardom (57.5kg). The gelding drew perfectly again in barrier 1; the plan was to race handily behind the leaders, saving ground against the rails. Happy Clapper was kept safe in the betting at $5.00, with the hardest to beat being the lightly-weighted three-year-olds Kementari ($3.20 fav) and D'Argento ($8.50).

Pat was more relaxed in the lead up in this race. 'We had won our Group 1 in the Epsom and then picked up a bonus in the Canterbury Stakes. And we weren't a $2.70 favourite this time.' Chrissy dropped Pat off at the races, once again resisting the chance to watch the Group 1 on track. 'See you after the race', she told Pat.

From his barrier, Happy Clapper took up a forward position on the rail as

Arbeitsam and Tom Melbourne came around to lead. The pace was quick up front, but Shinn had the Clapper perfectly balanced behind the leaders as they straightened, and surged him to the lead as Arbeitsam moved off the fence into the centre of the track. The going on the rails was good, and as Clapper quickened under Shinn's riding, Kementari was momentarily blocked between Arbeitsam and Tom Melbourne. Comin' Through ran on late but Happy Clapper had a decisive two length advantage on the line.

'Happy Clapper, the people's horse!' bellowed broadcaster Greg Radley. 'He hasn't dodged Winx, he's never run away from her and he's run second in two Doncasters … but today he claims one and it's all his.'

Arbeitsam held on for third from the fast finishing D'Argento. Kementari faded into sixth after having the wind knocked out of his sails, but Humidor and Tosen Stardom never came into the race. Tosen Stardom, which had jumped out of the ground to beat Happy Clapper the previous spring in the Emirates, finished second last and was immediately retired to stud.

Blake Shinn gave the huge crowd a salute after the line, turning the move into a Pete Townshend-inspired windmill punch to the heavens. 'What a ride by Shinn', Ron Dufficy enthused. 'He rode the rail and got the run at the right time. A dominant win.'

Shinn didn't need to move on the horse and yet the Clapper ran 1:33.17, the fastest Doncaster in history, and just 0.4 of a second outside Ike Dream's course record. Clearly emotional after the win, the jockey told broadcaster Bernadette Cooper on the way back to scale, 'That feels amazing … I just won the "Donny". He's so brave this horse; he's honest, he's tenacious, he's tough … well done to Pat Webster and his team.'

Back at winner's enclosure, Pat was besieged by well-wishers. 'The Doncaster was the race I always wanted to win, even as a kid', said Pat. 'Now I've done it.'

The jubilant trainer headed to the winner's lounge after the official presentations when his phone rang in the elevator. He looked at the number and answered the phone straight away. 'Some bloke in the lift commented, "That must be God for you to take a call at a moment like this".'

'Close enough,' the winner trainer remarked. It was Racing NSW CEO Peter V'landys ringing to congratulate him. 'That was great,' says Pat, 'that Peter took the time to call me after the race'.

Happy Clapper's win in the Doncaster Mile at his third attempt at the race was the good news story of the autumn. Racing journos and the general media had always supported Pat, and they got behind the veteran trainer who had finally found his champion horse. Racing NSW, giddy with the enormous success of Winx, were equally generous in their praise of the Webster team and their giant gelding. It was a win for the little guys in an increasingly competitive business.

The racing public had taken in Happy Clapper too. The gelding's fans were 'rusted on', as owner Michael Thomas knew they would be, proving that there was enough room in punters' hearts for Winx *and* Happy Clapper.

Pat Webster basked in the glory of his Doncaster victory, celebrating long into the night with family and friends, but on Monday morning it was back to work. When asked if Happy Clapper would take on Winx in the Group 1 Queen Elizabeth II Stakes (2000m), the buoyant trainer said there were '755,000 reasons' to back the horse up. That's how much prizemoney the race paid for second place.

'Blake Shinn was booked for Humidor so Kerrin McEvoy rode Happy Clapper. It was great theatre … the Sydney press billed it as "the showdown of the autumn", but the band played the same old song.'

Winx started at a prohibitive $1.24 favourite, with Happy Clapper the next best in the market at $11. The Clapper drew barrier 9 in the 10-horse field, his big race luck finally deserting him but, in fairness, Winx was drawn outside him and was the widest of the select field. Both horses went back in the early stages of the race, which is against Happy Clapper's preferred mode of racing, but whereas Winx had the ability to skirt the field with a blinding turn of foot, Happy Clapper was stuck on her inside and was dour in the run to the line.

The 2000m specialist Gailo Chop led the field into the straight, but Winx picked up the gelding just as easily, with Happy Clapper making ground along the rails to finish half a length third.

'Happy Clapper got too far back and should have run second, but Winx was far too good', Pat says. It was impossible for him to be disappointed after such a great autumn – Happy Clapper recorded two wins, a second and a third, all at Group 1 level, and won over $3.8 million in prizemoney in one preparation. It was a life changer for many associated with the horse, especially Pat.

'And who would have thought a lad from Inverell could be here doing that?'

***

After Happy Clapper's success in the 2018 Doncaster Mile, Pat's neighbour John Singleton rang the Websters' Kulnura farm. 'Has Pat celebrated his Doncaster success yet?' an immediately recognisable voice asked Chrissy Webster when she picked up the home phone.

'Yes', Chrissy told Singo. 'We all went out to dinner.'

'No, has he *really* celebrated?' Singo asked. The former adman, racehorse breeder and long-time stable supporter felt that Pat hadn't received the accolades he deserved for winning the Doncaster Mile. He would like to do something for Pat.

'I was having a drink with Singo at his farm on the NSW Central Coast one day', Pat says. 'He was complaining there was nowhere that he could get a good coffee in the morning so he was going to buy a nursery down the road and build a restaurant there with a rail out the front so he could go down there for a coffee and tie his horse up.'

Twelve months later, John Singleton opened his restaurant, which he named 'Saddles', at nearby Mount White. The 10-hectare property includes a nursery, bakehouse and an eatery, which takes its inspiration from Heath Harris, an artisan saddler who has worked with Singo at his Strawberry Hills Stud and who designed unique saddle chairs for the dining room's brass-scalloped bar.

To honour Pat and his training achievement, Singo invited a cross-section of Sydney's racing identities, including journos Ian McNeice, Greg Radley, Ray Thomas and Max Presnell and special guest Chris Waller, to a celebratory lunch at Saddles. 'All the blokes who started out with Pat in the 1970s', Singo says.

'Singo sent out taxis and limos for everybody. It was a race day Wednesday, but they all turned up to hear Chris and me talk about how we met, our respective careers and the rivalry between Happy Clapper and Winx.'

Waller had a big team in at Warwick Farm that day, and the assembled racing crowd watched on a TV monitor as his horses won the first three races. 'Chris Waller turned to Singo and said, "Mr Singleton, this is Pat's day. Let's turn the TV off." It didn't worry me, everyone was enjoying themselves, but Chris was adamant.' The Waller stable trained five winners that day but the focus was on Pat.

'We were talking about Racing Mates and certain charities we support so Chris said let's get a photo of Winx and Happy Clapper in the George Ryder Stakes and we'll all sign it … you, me, Blake and Hughie.'

Sometime later, multiple copies of the 2018 George Ryder finish arrived at Pat's farm, the image already signed in each corner by Waller, Bowman and Shinn. After Pat signed his name, the pictures were framed by Waller who sent his long-time friend six copies to give away to charity.

'It's a great piece of memorabilia,' says Pat. 'It actually looks like the Clapper is ahead of Winx, but then it's just the angle of the picture.

'And we all know what happened at the finish, don't we?'

CHAPTER 18

Two and Two is Almost Five

There's a long-held belief in racing that a training master must ensure their jockey is 'early to bed and early to rise, and sees who picks them up and takes them to go to the races, and knows the company they keep on a Saturday night'.

Pat Webster has always had a special affinity for jockeys. The obvious reason is because he started out as an apprentice jockey in the bush and knows how hard the life is, but it's also because he has always had an eye out for the little guys trying to make a go of it in a very tough sport.

'It's just in my nature', Pat says. 'That's why I take on kids who had problems and nobody else wanted.'

A lot of trainers don't want kids anymore, he says. 'They haven't got the time and don't want the trouble', Pat once observed. 'Kids must have that hint of rogue to begin with … the trouble is bridling it.'

Pat was in the trainer's hut at Randwick one morning when he met two young boys who wanted to become jockeys. One was Marlon Dolendo, a Philippine migrant, and the other was an Australian lad, as Pat says, 'covered head to toe in tattoos and piercings'.

'I asked Marlon if he had ever ridden a horse', Pat remembers. 'He said, "No, only water buffalo".' Pat took him on and sent the other boy up to his brothers in law, Jim and Greg Lee. Marlon Dolendo worked hard and succeeded, the other boy didn't.

'Marlon rode some good winners for me, but he thought he had the flu and was actually suffering from kidney failure. His sister donated a kidney for him and Racing NSW arranged for his aunty to come and visit him from the Philippines.' Dolendo later moved to the North Coast of NSW, and works for Racing NSW as a liaison with other Filipino jockeys.

Joey Galea was another case in hand. 'Neville Begg had shown Joey the ropes before he came to my stable. Joey had wanted to be a jockey so badly, he wagged school and could barely read and write when he left in Year 8.'

Pat encouraged Joey to do a literacy and numeracy course at a nearby TAFE. He did so well he was conscripted to give Marlon Dolendo lessons.

'It took a lot of guts and determination to do what he did', Pat says. Galea also had that touch of rogue about him that Pat talks about. He once called out to Pat in front of pressmen, 'Do you want me for At Sea on Saturday boss? Because if you don't, Mr Cummings might want me for one of his goodies'. Joey ended up being one of the leading riders in the NSW Western Districts before moving back to Malta to live.

Chris Whalan was still a 4kg claiming apprentice at the age of twenty-one when he came to the Webster stables. Pat pressed racing authorities to extend his apprenticeship period so he could outride his allowance and finish his HSC at the nearby TAFE. Whalan was aboard the fabulously named Chokito when the Webster-trained horse won at Rosehill one day at 200/1.

'I remember I had $4 the place on it', Pat says. 'The owner had $2 each way.' Whalan worked hard for Pat, but tired of the racing life and turned his back on the sport. 'I inherited Shane Arnold from Taree and then gave Matt Privato a start. Shane could ride, and Matty later went to TJ Smith and rode with great success, which didn't worry me because I'd done my bit. He was a beautiful kid.'

Pat always got the best out of his young charges. 'You get more out of people throwing sugar instead of salt', he says. 'We used the wheelie bins on course to collect horse manure at the stable. I told my boys to go and get a bin and where did they get it from? It was (chief steward) Ray Murrihy's wheelie bin. "Take it back, take it back", I told them. These little guys were running up Doncaster Ave laughing.'

Pat cares about his jockeys as people, not products. 'I worried about them because I become very close to them', he says. It's still the same today with the work he does with jockeys around the state in his role as a drugs and alcohol counsellor for Racing NSW. 'How do you deal with their issues if you don't become close? You have to get close to them to get inside their heads.'

In 2018, jockey Jackson Morris contacted Pat and asked for another stint as stable rider. The young jockey, who had ridden Shy Hero to victory in the TJ Smith Stakes almost twenty years ago, was on another comeback trail after increasing weight and lack of opportunity in Queensland saw him take out a greyhound trainer's licence.

Back in Sydney, Jackson was put on a retainer as a trackwork rider for Pat, and also picked up rides for Jim and Greg Lee and trainer John Thompson. 'He was really dedicated for a time, but we've since had a parting of the ways. Jackson burns a lot of bridges wherever he goes', but there is a fondness there too.

'Chrissy's nephew, (jockey) Jason Lee, calls me Uncle Pat so Jackson starting calling me Uncle Pat as well.'

The top jockeys aren't missed either. 'I like to take the mickey out of them so they don't get big heads', Pat says. 'I've known Hughie Bowman since he was an apprentice at Bathurst. Hughie sat three wide on one of my horses at Wyong one day and got beat. "I could have ridden that to win", I told him. I give it to Corey Brown every chance I get. And Glenn Boss.'

And the apple doesn't fall far from the tree. When Wayne Webster and jockey Glen Boss disagreed over riding tactics, Wayne told the three-time Melbourne Cup winner, 'Your name's Boss but I'm the boss around here. And Bruce Springsteen trumps the pair of us'.

Pat is always ready to give a jockey a reality check. Been there, done that.

But young jockeys are especially vulnerable, he says, because most leave home at a young age and are often poorly educated. 'Before you know it, there are "new" friends and hangers-on, and the jockey starts to think, well "two and two is almost five". They start cutting corners and making poor decisions in their lives, and before they know it, their careers are over.'

It's a perfect storm Pat Webster has witnessed time and time again in his career as a jockey and trainer – jockeys getting ahead of themselves when they become successful and making poor decisions. And all too quickly, their career is over – increasing weight, a bad fall, a suspension or lack of opportunities as a senior jockey.

Pat was always passionate about the establishment of an Australian Racing and Equine Academy. 'This is something that is more important than any grandstands or "theatre of the horse"', he said way back in 1997. 'It is about the future of our industry ... we need this for all the kids coming through. We've got to have a home for them where they can sit down in class and not be like gypsies. We need to get on to teaching these kids.'

But still jockeys fell through the cracks. Melbourne apprentice Daniel Ganderton wasted thousands of dollars on alcohol and turned his back on the sport to reclaim his health. Mitch Beadman wasted his immense talent and, although he no longer rides, he has reclaimed his health. Josh Adams rode the racing roller-coaster ... success, suspension, drug addiction, serious injury.

Even leading senior jockeys have had their well-publicised public struggles with drugs, alcohol and gambling, so it was clear something more needed to be done by racing officials. Maurice Logue knew of Pat's dealings with son Patrick, and believed the racing industry could benefit from that sort of personal experience. Chief Executive of Racing NSW Peter V'landys quickly jumped on board. Would Pat mentor young jockeys around the state?

'Mine is a very hard-earned experience', Pat says. 'It's not something you can learn or buy.' So, for the past decade, he has devoted himself to helping others, travelling all over country NSW to talk to jockeys, young and old, about the dangers of drugs.

Peter V'landys suggested it would be best if Pat completed the required counselling courses. 'There was the real fear that some in the industry would say, "What does he bloody know? He's just a horse trainer"', says Pat. He undertook a course in drug, alcohol and mental illness under the guidance of Maurice Logue and Keith Bullock of Racing NSW, and Robyn Parkinson at Hawkesbury TAFE, having just recovered himself from major back surgery.

What was it like going back to school at almost sixty years of age? 'It was terrible, just like I remembered, but I knew I had to do it. The last session I had was one-on-one with a tutor inside a glass cubicle, and I said at the end, "How did I go?" The guy said, "I don't know if you took a lot out of it but it's the best session I've ever had. I learned a lot". Everything he knew was just theory, but when I told him about my experiences with Patrick, he actually learned something.

'But I'm not an instant expert … (and) if I can help one kid, I've done my job.'

Mentoring comes naturally to Pat. 'People can see if you're bunging it on', he says. 'They take the first meeting out of respect, and the success of Happy Clapper has helped in building that respect', he admits.

Pat holds mandatory workshops for apprentice jockeys in each region of NSW, which involve intensive discussions about the dangers and effects of alcohol and drug use. While the workshops are mandatory for apprentice jockeys, other industry participants are also encouraged to attend.

Pat gets wind of a jockey struggling with drugs all the time, both formal and informal; a phone call in the middle of the night, or Racing NSW will ring him and he will follow up. 'Even if I don't know the jockey personally, I will ring and introduce myself, then arrange to meet them.'

He also holds group sessions with apprentices at six major centres around NSW each year. 'Places like Wagga Wagga, Canberra, Grafton, Port Macquarie – and any stable hands who want to come are welcome too.'

The sessions can become emotionally charged. 'We operate like any drugs and alcohol session; we sit in a circle and share stories … I tell them my story, then they tell me theirs.' Sitting in a circle breaks down barriers, he says. 'Usually I leave a box of tissues in the middle of the circle, because we will need them.'

'You have to get them talking. Only then you can understand where they are coming from and the issues they face.'

Other than access to drugs and too much money, the big threat to jockeys is falling in with the wrong crowd. 'The thing I consistently say to young jockeys is mix with your childhood mates; the ones who knew you before you were famous, not the blokes you met two weeks ago who are now hanging off your coat-tails.'

When pressed, Pat can identify one common denominator in most of the drug cases he has been involved in, including his own son: 'That one bad apple who ruins the box', he says. 'That one "friend" who takes advantage of them.'

Some people on the fringes of the racing game will use any information they can get to make a buck and these kids are naïve and vulnerable, Pat says. 'All of a sudden, they're in the limelight and they're riding winners. The bloke who wants to use them will always be able find them.'

Pat tells the kids he mentors bluntly: lay down with dogs you'll get up with fleas. '"Who are you mixing with?" I ask them. At the end of the day, it's the people they associate with who they think are their friends who will get them into the most trouble … they're out at a party, and they don't have to be jockeys, it can be any kid in any suburb, and they'll be introduced to drugs.'

Obviously, some kids are more easily influenced than others. 'When I work with a jockey one on one, I go right back into their history', Pat says.

'Plenty of kids have gone through a tough upbringing or a broken home, and that with the added pressure of the racing game they can be easily sucked in.'

Alcohol is the worse drug there is, Pat believes. 'Would a kid take an "eccy" pill at a party if they weren't full of alcohol? Probably not. We're all vulnerable when we have too much alcohol but it's not going to be banned, is it? It's a primer for a lot of bad decisions people make … drink-driving, domestic abuse, sexual assault. And if the kids already have underlying problems, it's like throwing petrol on a fire.'

The same thing happens in other sports, notably rugby league. 'Sometimes more so', Pat says. 'But for jockeys, riding in a race is like a drug for them too. It's intoxicating having control of a 500kg beast underneath you. It's not really about the money, it's about the competition. But the money is a corrupting influence. Many young jockeys find success, but they have so little experience handling money they quickly get into trouble.'

By far the biggest issue at the moment is the availability of methamphetamine, more commonly known as 'ice'. And as racing authorities have long known, ice is an appetite suppressant. And it has less calories than alcohol for a much bigger high.

'Ice is obviously a problem right across society', Pat says. 'Some shearers in the bush are on ice because they can shear more sheep while under the influence. And yet they'll come out and say to the press, "There are no drugs in shearing". That's a perfect example of burying your head in the sand.'

Racing NSW is taking a proactive approach. Recently Pat was contacted by the mother of a former leading jockey. She was giving her son $160 a week to make ends meet, but the hoop was living in his car and spending the money on drugs. Pat knew the young man was on drugs as soon as he talked to him – he had seen the tell-tale signs before with his own son. After liaising with Racing NSW, emergency accommodation was secured for the jockey, with the bond and eight weeks rent paid in advance, while he gained professional help.

Sometimes, young jockeys find it easier to speak to an 'outsider' like Pat rather than a family member about their issues – there's just too much shame and emotion involved. Thinking of his own family experience, he adds, 'If I had someone to help us from outside the home, the outcome would have been different'.

Pat pulls no punches in his dealings with jockeys. He is no easy touch. 'When I shut the door, I tell them how it really is. "You're all reading your own press and you're acting like a bunch of big heads so stop being fucking idiots." I'm not standing at a whiteboard with a pointer saying, "Now boys and girls, cocaine is a dangerous drug …"'

They are told 'peer to peer' what they need to do to stay safe and be successful. 'That's the level they operate on, "mate to mate". They don't need a pompous do-gooder telling them what to do.' And dropping a 'fuck' every now and then helps, Pat says. 'At least they're not nodding off to sleep. When you talk like an ex-painter and docker, they listen.'

And Pat brings something else to the table after a lifetime in the industry. 'I can also help with their riding technique, life issues and even represent them at racing inquiries.'

A good country jockey had been dodging and weaving stewards, trying not to get caught using drugs until, of course, he was caught and suspended. 'I believe he wanted to get caught', Pat says. 'After I worked with him, he said, "Pat, I'm going to come back a better rider" and I told him, "Don't worry about that. You have to be a better a person … your fellow riders think you're arrogant and you knock them down in races. You have to wise up".'

The jockey is now back riding plenty of winners and, more importantly, is happy in his craft. 'And he can always call me whenever he needs to', Pat says.

Pat will continue working in the role for Racing NSW too for as long as they need him, but he has no doubt about the importance of the work he is doing. 'These guys not only have their own lives in their hands but the lives of their racing comrades at stake too.'

When Jockeys ride in a race their decision-making skills have to be 'spot on', Pat says. 'Then they come off the track and make really dumb decisions in their personal life. We can't let that happen because if they are under the influence of drugs or affected by alcohol, they might be racing the next day and they have to be on their game, for their safety and the safety of others.'

Young jockeys need to be able to break the cycle, and Pat's here to help them do that. 'There's so much talent that goes to waste and sometimes you just need to spend a bit more time with them', he told journalist Andrew Webster in 2018.

'It's a bit like working with Happy Clapper. The challenge is to unlock the talent – not just acknowledge it's there.'

CHAPTER 19

You've Been Winxed

Happy Clapper is like one of the family to trainer Pat Webster. Having made the decision to base the gelding in Melbourne for his 2018 spring campaign and have another crack at Winx in the WS Cox Plate, Pat treated his stable star to two new rugs.

'When I go to the horse store, I can't help myself', Pat admits. 'It's like buying for the grandkids. My wife looked at me and asked, "why buy the horse two new rugs?"

'He's won three Group 1s, that's why.'

But the gelding's preparation hit an early hurdle.

'I wasn't happy with the Clapper's trials', Pat admits. 'In my own heart I thought I would put blinkers back on him in his second trial but Blake was pretty happy when he finished fourth over 1250m on the Kensington track.'

Shinn was then badly injured in a fall in a trial later that day. Taken to nearby Prince of Wales Hospital where X-rays revealed he had fractures in his C1 and C3 vertebra, the Melbourne Cup-winning jockey faced a long recovery.

'Blake was injured, another bad omen', Pat says, who booked experienced Melbourne jockey Michael Zahra to ride Happy Clapper in Melbourne.

The first run in Melbourne was in the Group 1 Memsie Stakes at Caulfield. 'He wasn't right in the coat, which I really go on, but his run was bloody disgraceful. The Clapper struggled to get around the track but if you watch the race, the last 50m was the best part of the run so we were hopeful he would improve.'

The gelding's next start, in the Group 1 Makybe Diva Stakes (1600m) at Flemington a fortnight later, resulted in a close fifth behind Grunt, beaten less than three lengths after copping a bad check at the 200m. 'The young course announcer got excited, "Look how Happy Clapper's finished it off", but I still wasn't happy.'

Then the horse bled.

'If blood comes out of one of the nostrils, a horse isn't banned. But two nostrils? They're banned for three months because the blood has come from the lungs.' If a horse suffers two bleeding attacks during their career, they're banned for life. The gelding's future was now in the balance.

'We'd put the Clapper on a blood thinner because it helped his joints. I think it may have thinned his blood too much. Since he bled, the Clapper hasn't had that medication and he's gone pretty good.'

While Winx was tempting history by trying to win a record fourth WS Cox Plate, Happy Clapper was resting up at the Westers' Kulnura property. During that long summer of recovery, Blake Shinn, another injured champion, came up to the farm to visit the now eight-year-old gelding.

Shinn liked what he saw.

***

The sleepless nights began again for Pat Webster straight after Happy Clapper came back into work at the beginning of 2019. The pressure on the horse to come back from a bleeding attack was felt by the entire stable, which went into 'Clapper mode' as soon the gelding walked back on Randwick racecourse.

'The Clapper doesn't need a lot of work', Pat says. 'Racing people would be shocked how little hard galloping we give him.' Apprentice jockey Jacob Gilchrist helped Ainsley Fox work with Happy Clapper each day and the horse maintained a strict afternoon routine that had been so successful for him.

Happy Clapper was in good condition after his enforced layoff, but Pat needed to know early in the campaign if the old gelding could stand up to the rigors of racing. 'There had been plenty of hard times with the horse,' Pat told a willing press contingent, 'but he's come back as strong as he's ever been. Our worry is not that he wins, but that he finishes his racing career safely after the bleeding attack.'

After the bleeding attack, Pat opted to take regular blood tests and scope the horse after each trial. 'Happy Clapper's red blood cells are always down. When you take the blood, he's always relaxed. Apparently, he stores a lot of red blood cells in his spleen and they are only released when he gets excited.'

In January, Blake Shinn rode Happy Clapper over 900m on the Randwick track, squeezing the horse through a series of gaps into fourth position, two and a half lengths behind the winner. 'The horse had a good blow after the trial,' Pat says, 'but his recovery was quick'.

Two weeks later, Happy Clapper defeated noted sprinters Special Missile and I am Excited over 1000m at Randwick. This second trial topped the Clapper off for his return to racing in the Group 2 Apollo Stakes (1400m) at Randwick in February.

And another showdown with Winx.

The Winx juggernaut had rolled on since the pair had last met in the 2018 Queen Elizabeth Stakes the previous autumn. During the spring of 2018, Winx won four more Group 1s – a third straight Warwick Stakes (1400m), a third straight George Main Stakes (1600m), a second Turnbull

Stakes (2000m) and a record fourth consecutive WS Cox Plate (2040m). When the mare's connections announced this preparation would be her last before being retired to stud, the wonder mare had won twenty-nine consecutive races, including twenty-two at Group 1 level.

Blake Shinn was unavailable through suspension for the Clapper's return date with Winx in the Apollo Stakes so Pat, with Michael Thomas' blessing, entrusted the ride to Sam Clipperton. For the previous two and a half years Clipperton had ridden with success in Hong Kong, but before hopping aboard the Clapper on race day, he had never even sat on the horse.

In a good omen, Clipperton rode talented mare Eckstein to a surprise win in the Group 3 Southern Cross Stakes (1200m) in the race before the Apollo Stakes. Clipperton then jumped Happy Clapper from barrier 1 and sat outside the leader, the gelding's old Epsom rival Tom Melbourne. Winx was well back, fifth on the outside of the eight runners, but within sight of the leaders with Hugh Bowman sitting patiently. Tom Melbourne dropped off at the top of the straight, so Clipperton moved the Clapper to the lead at the 300m mark. At this point, Bowman had brought Winx around the field and was quickly reeling in Happy Clapper.

'Winx looks like she's struggling but when she gets past them it's like another gear', Pat observed after the race. The winning margin wasn't great – just 2.3 lengths, but the Clapper defeated the rest of the field just as easily, with another four lengths back to third placed Egg Tart. As Pat told journalist Ray Thomas after the race, '(My) horse is a champion in his own right and he ran accordingly but Winx was just too good'.

'We were over the moon with Happy Clapper's first run after his bleeding attack. The horse ran great fresh, first up, and I was a very proud old trainer when he finished second.'

Happy Clapper and Winx next clashed in the 1600m Group 1 Chipping Norton Stakes at Randwick. Again, Pat dared to dream. But how could he turn the tables on the wonder mare?

Only five other runners took on Winx and Happy Clapper in the Chelmsford, and four had finished well behind the pair in the Apollo Stakes. Libran, like the other four runners, was a stayer getting ready to peak later in their preparations, and all were trained by Winx's mentor, Chris Waller. Happy Clapper was the outsider to the Waller team.

'They weren't going to take the mare on,' says Pat, 'so that left us.'

Pat hatched a plan with jockey Blake Shinn in an attempt to end Winx's winning run. 'I was working with the apprentices at Wyong on the Thursday before the race, and I sat down with Blake and had a couple of words with him. There was no speed in the race and Winx might be vulnerable second up.'

'I think we can knock her off', Blake told the trainer.

'There was no leader in the race, so we'd have to lead', Pat said. 'Clapper had never led before in a race but here he was, an eight-year-old taking on Winx. It was crazy.'

Sam Clipperton had to hold Happy Clapper together in the Apollo, but Blake said he'd increase the tempo from the 1000m and try and steal the race.

'Well, can you make it the 700m because this is not his grand final', Pat countered. 'That's confidence for you … but I was really thinking, "You're dreaming son". At the end of the day I didn't think we could beat her so let's try for a good second.'

Pat was in the stalls at Randwick on race day – Happy Clapper positioned opposite Winx – which were besieged by people trying to get a good look at the mare. Many race fans wandered over to Pat, including Winx's high-profile owners, to wish him luck.

'Some people wanted to see Winx get beat', Pat says. 'Its human nature I guess, but I'm not one of them. It would be like killing Bambi.'

Winx was going for a world record 23rd Group 1 victory and a huge crowd was on track that day. Form analysts had worked out that Happy

Clapper would need to lead to have any chance of turning the tables on the champion, but when Pat spotted one of the ATC stewards early on the big day, he couldn't resist making a little mischief.

'A change of riding tactics on Happy Clapper', Pat informed the steward. 'We are going to ride the Clapper quietly from behind.'

The steward was ashen-faced. 'Mr Webster, I hope you're joking.' Pat opened up with a broad smile.

When the field jumped, Happy Clapper went straight to the lead. 'He's never led in his life,' course broadcaster Darren Flindell declared, 'but he's two lengths clear at the 1200m'. Winx was fourth on the outside in great position, but by the 600m Happy Clapper had extended the lead to five lengths.

'This has the crowd on the edge of their seats.'

On the turn, Winx had moved into second place, still four lengths behind the Clapper but jockey Hugh Bowman's elbows were pumping. For a fleeting moment she looked to be in trouble, just as she had on many other occasions during her career, but in an instant, she had the race won. The mare took the lead at the 120m and won by just under two lengths, but the Clapper had made it exciting. They had made a race of it.

'Winx is amazing … she can cover all bases, this mare', Pat told journalist Ben Zerafa after the race. 'Blake really made it a test today … that was the plan. It turned out to be a really good plan until the 200m mark. At least we had a throw at the stumps.'

Pat even admitted that he wasn't even watching Happy Clapper in the run – like the rest of Australia, he only had eyes for Winx. 'If you watch the replay, at the 700m you would have thought she was out of business.'

Except this was *Winx*.

'We could have sat and had a cosy run and looked for second place but that was not in his makeup. I've been around racing for more than fifty years … I've watched thousands of races and I can tell when a jockey is kidding to them. I saw Hughie Bowman getting stuck into her and when she came back underneath him, I knew he had us covered. Clapper was a long way in front but I was just looking at Hughie's elbows.'

It was this race, more than any other, that endeared the Clapper to the hard-nosed Australian racing public. Webster realised that people loved his horse too and respected the fact that he was willing to have a crack at the mare, time and time again, when so many other horses were home in their stalls.

'I walked into the Newcastle jockey room and Grant Buckley said, "Good on you, Pat." Shaun Guymer told me it was just as good as winning.' Almost.

'Winx had to run a record time to catch him', Pat says. 'A rising 8-year old mare ran the fastest 1400m ever in the Apollo, the fastest ever 1600m in the Chipping Norton, and completed unbelievable sectionals. Winx was getting older but instead of getting slower, like most other horse, she was actually *better* with age. That was the scary part.'

But even with Winx placed on a pedestal where she truly belonged, Happy Clapper has found his own place as a public favourite. 'Winx is a champion, but my bloke's a champion too.'

Pat hoped the race would not take its toll on his horse for the rest of the autumn. 'Chris Waller even texted me after the Chipping Norton. "How did your horse pull up?" He's a tough old bastard.'

It had always been Pat's hope to have another crack at the Doncaster before he was weighted out of the race. The ATC handicapper gave Happy Clapper 59kg, but there was another option that year: the introduction of the All-Star Mile (1600m) – a newly minted Melbourne race worth $5 million where the majority of runners were selected by popular vote. The horses with the top ten votes, plus four wildcards selected by Racing Victoria, made up the field that would tackle the Flemington event in this the inaugural running of the race.

Happy Clapper is arguably the best miler in Australia, although Melbourne had always presented problems for him. When racing discussions turned to the gelding's lack of success in Melbourne, Pat rightly pointed out that Clapper was Group 1 placed at Flemington. 'It's not Randwick,' Pat would tease, 'but it'll do'.

The problem remained, however. Happy Clapper was not guaranteed a spot in the race.

When Pat and Wayne Webster fronted the media, usually to discuss Winx, they'd quickly add, 'and don't forget to vote for Happy Clapper in the All-Star Mile ... he's the people's horse'. In the end, Racing Victoria exercised its discretionary powers and selected Happy Clapper as one of their wildcard entries.

Trainer James Cummings boosted the standard of the field by putting forward his pair, Hartnell and Alizee, but most punters saw the race as a showdown between Happy Clapper and Group 1-winning Tasmanian filly Mystic Journey. Pat and Chrissy's granddaughter Kate Vance pulled out the lucky No.1 at the All-Star Mile barrier draw. The first person to congratulate the lass and her proud mother Diane was James Cummings.

The Happy Clapper team was confident in the run, with Happy Clapper settling well for regular jockey Blake Shinn, one out and one back in fourth place. 'Blake had him beautifully positioned and was just about to let him go when: "oh shit, there's nothing there".' The horse struggled from the 300m mark, rallying again on the line to finish eighth, four lengths from the winner Mystic Journey.

Pat and Bale Shinn were dumbfounded after the run. When the horse was scoped after the race, it was discovered that Happy Clapper had bled internally. 'If you scoped ten horses after a hard run, seven of them will be found to have bled internally', Pat says, but at least the horse had not bled through the nostrils.

A fourth straight tilt at the Doncaster Mile was now out of the question, but if the horse recovered in time, Happy Clapper could take on Winx in her farewell to racing, in the Queen Elizabeth II Stakes at the end of the Sydney carnival.

Winx geared up for her final race with another Group 1 win in the George Ryder Stakes (1500m) at Rosehill. A heavy 8 track couldn't slow the mare, defeating subsequent Doncaster Mile winner Brutal by three lengths. Happy Clapper faced his moment of truth in a 1200m trial, far away from the media spotlight. Would the gelding race on, be sent for a spell or perhaps even retired?

Racenet's Clinton Payne reported: 'Popular galloper Happy Clapper showed his appreciation for being back home in Sydney when coming from well back, without any pressure from Blake Shinn, to reel in the leaders in his 1200m trial'. The Clapper would fight on.

At an official ATC function to promote the Queen Elizabeth II, Pat told a packed audience from on stage, 'I'm here to throw the white flag up … I don't have the Clapper where I want him after the Melbourne run, so we're running for the minor prize money'.

The Q&A that night turned to the observation that horses tended not to bounce back after being 'Winxed'. Black Caviar had Hay List, Winx had Happy Clapper. That's what the press was saying. Whereas Hay List was never the same horse after taking on Black Caviar too many times, Happy Clapper kept coming back at the mare.

'With every hero you need a villain,' says Pat, 'but Clapper's a hero too'. The media called it 'The Winx Factor' – not only does she beat her opponents, but she also breaks their hearts. All except Happy Clapper, and to a lesser degree, Hartnell.

'Honestly, I do feel sorry for the horses chasing her', Pat admitted. 'Twice we had her where we wanted her, in the 2016 Doncaster and 2017 George Ryder. If she had any weaknesses, we would have beaten her then. Let me tell you, she hasn't any.'

Winx lined up for her final race with Royal Randwick packed in excess of 43,000 fans. Happy Clapper and Hartnell took their place in the field, alongside Japanese import Kluger, and would fill out the minor placings behind the great mare. Starting a $1.06 favourite – Phar Lap odds for anyone old enough to remember – Winx made a long sweeping run on the outside of Happy Clapper as the field rounded the corner and surged away to complete the fairytale. Kluger was second, Hartnell third and the Clapper holding on for fourth, beaten about 6 lengths.

It was the mare's 33rd consecutive win, her 25th Group 1 success, and 20th victory at Randwick ... all world records. It was also the 100th Group 1 win in trainer Chris Waller's phenomenal career.

Pat Webster is immensely proud of his horse, and rightly so. 'We are part of the Winx Story,' he says, 'and happy to be mentioned in the same breath'. As his daughter Diane pointed out to him recently, fifty years from now when they show Winx's highlights reel Happy Clapper will be there too, chasing her home.

A minor support role in the greatest story of the Australian turf.

'That makes me feel good', says Pat.

Jack's Story

On Good Friday in 1999, Pat and Chrissy Webster received a phone call from the two men who had bought their liquor shop in Maroubra. 'A young woman has overdosed on a cocktail of drugs and is being loaded into an ambulance', they said. 'The problem was, she has a baby in a bassinet and the paramedics have no way of safely transporting the infant to the hospital.

'Pat, we think it's your grandson.'

It was the phone call Pat and Chrissy had dreaded, but they knew immediately what they had to do.

When Patrick Jnr was in his early 20s, he formed a relationship with a woman who had gone to school with his younger sister, Diane. After meeting again at a party, they began dating and using drugs together. 'Patrick really loved her,' Chrissy Webster says, 'even when she was using during her pregnancy. But then, both of them could not make the right decisions in the state they were in'.

The first Pat and Chrissy knew they had a grandchild was when they saw Patrick Jnr pushing an old stroller down the street with a baby in it. 'He was off his head, even then', Pat says, and within weeks his eldest son was back in gaol. Mother and child were living in a housing commission home at Woolloomooloo, Patrick's partner having taken up with another drug user while he was in gaol.

Pat was so concerned about the infant, as yet unnamed, that he tracked down mother and child through a network of friends and acquaintances, and went to check on them. 'The baby was covered in mosquito bites on his face and arms', Pat remembers. 'Sitting on a chair looking at him in his bassinet, the baby had a look on his face as if to say, "Please get me out of here". I went home to Chrissy and said "I can't leave that child there".'

Chrissy asked her husband what he wanted to do. 'I'm going to go and get him and bring him back here', he told her.

'Chrissy said, "Pat, you can't do that".

'"But Christine," I told her, "his brown eyes were following me all around the room". I just couldn't leave him there …'

Pat went over to the apartment the next morning with a family friend. 'We brought him home here and cleaned him up.' Chrissy named him Jack Leslie Webster after Pat's grandfather, Jack Burns, and Pat's dad 'Spider'.

The baby's mother trusted Pat and Chrissy. She called Pat 'Poddy' and he was the first person she turned to when she got into trouble. The Websters helped her out financially, because she was the mother of their grandchild and, also, it's in their nature to help.

Pat and Chrissy looked after the infant for three weeks to give the mother a break, and then reluctantly gave the baby back to her. Then came the phone call on Good Friday to come and rescue the boy. That made their minds up, pretty much then and there. They would raise their grandson as their own. There would be no handing him back anymore.

'I never wanted to do it, raising another child in my forties', Pat admits. 'But we had to do something.'

'It was a big commitment', Chrissy remembers. 'I was unsure at first, but Pat is a beautiful and generous man. "That's your grandson," he said to me, "and if we don't give him a life, he won't have one. And we can give him a good life".'

The Websters gained permission from the baby's mother to do a DNA check on the child. 'He didn't look like any of us … red hair, "pale as" complexion,' says Pat, 'so we did the DNA.' The baby was Patrick's son.

'We asked Terence Tobin QC to put our case forward to the courts to look after the child. Jack's mother said she was happy for "Mr and Mrs Webster" to look after the baby, and we've had him ever since.'

Jack has had no contact with his mother, and only a tenuous relationship with Patrick because his father was in and out of gaol during his childhood. 'We're nan and pop, and mum and dad', says Chrissy.

The Websters started the difficult task of parenting again in their late 40s. 'Carrying a bassinet in to a restaurant was tricky', Pat laughs. 'Chrissy used to drop the word "grandparents" into a lot of our conversations because I didn't want people to think I had got myself a mail order bride with a baby in tow.'

But parenting, fourth time around, was a revelation. 'I loved every second of it', says Pat.

Not that it was always easy. 'When we first got Jack as a baby, we took him to our farm at Mudgee and he cried all the way there. And it's a long fucking way to Mudgee, let me tell you.'

'We were totally honest with him', says Chrissy. "You know Jack, if there's anything you want to know about your parents you only have to ask", I told him. "We don't want you to be angry with them."

'"Angry? Why would I be angry with them?" he said. "They left me alone to live my life."'

'It's funny when you're raising someone else's child', Chrissy says. 'You can never fill the void that's missing but we did the best we could. As I explained to my other children, "You go to bed at night and kiss and cuddle your children goodnight. Well, Jack doesn't get that".'

When he was old enough, Jack went to the same primary school as the other Webster children before going to Waverley Junior School for Years 5 and 6. High school constituted another big decision to be made. The Websters sent Jack to boarding school at St Joseph's, Hunter's Hill.

'It was always our intention to send Jack to boarding school', Pat says. 'We prepared him for it all through junior school. We said to him that he needed boarding school. When he asked why, we said because it's the best thing for you … you'll love it, you'll make a lot of friends, and it will be the best years of your life. And you'll always have that connection with the people you meet there.'

'It was a case of allowing him the space to grow up', says Chrissy. 'We gave it a lot of thought. He has no siblings, and with Pat and me being older, it was important that Jack was able to stand on his own two feet.'

The plan was to make the boy self-sufficient. They weren't going to be around forever, Pat and Chrissy told him. 'But you have to have the right person to go through with the plan, and Jack was that person', Pat says. 'It almost broke my heart to leave him there but he came home on holidays and was a model student. He was given an opportunity and he took it with both hands.'

'I trusted their decision', Jack Webster, now twenty, says. 'I knew that they were doing it from a position of love and it ended up being the best thing for me. I was raised as an only child, the centre of my own little world. At boarding school, I had to live in a dorm with other boys, eat breakfast with them and share a bathroom with them. It was good for me because it taught me independence. I loved every aspect of boarding school … the curriculum, the sport and social sides of things.'

There is a sense of great pride and accomplishment with Pat and Chrissy that they guided Jack through his teenage years. 'Jack left no stone unturned with his schooling', says Pat. 'He played union when he didn't want to because he's not a tough guy; he got into rowing, he was competitive and academic. It was one of the proudest days of my life when he graduated in 2018.'

Jack is now at Notre Dame University in Sydney, studying Psychology and Counselling. 'I've always been interested in human behaviour', Jack says. 'Why people do certain things, it's all still a mystery. We can't really explain why we feel some way, or believe certain things or say certain things. It's going to be interesting to study that.'

He also has a passion for film, and filmmaking, and enjoys making short films with his friends. Perhaps an entry in the Tropfest competition is on the cards.

'That's the goal', he says.

Find something you love, do it and you never work a day in your life, his grandfather once told him. It could sum up Pat's life as well.

'When Jack went for his interview at Notre Dame, I suggested that he mention Terry Tobin QC, who was previously Chancellor of the University and remains a close family friend. Jack said, "Pop, I'd really like to do this on my own", which made me feel really proud he had the confidence in himself. When they saw his paperwork with a reference from Terry, who has known Jack all his life, they quickly piped up, 'Why didn't you tell us you knew Mr Tobin?"'

Terry and Bernadette Tobin first met Pat and Chrissy Webster when he operated a spelling paddock on the NSW Central Coast. As a boy, Tobin grew up near Flemington racecourse and dreamed of winning a Melbourne Cup. 'I raced a few horses, and bred a couple. Pat trained for me too as well, but none so memorable that I can remember their names.'

The Tobins could relate immediately to Pat and Chrissy, even though they have different backgrounds, occupations and come from different states. 'Pat is a completely honest and truthful man and Chrissy tells it as it is.' Over the years, he has acted for Pat in a couple of court cases and even provided evidence to support a character reference for Pat's son Patrick. He's also had a bit to do with Jack Webster.

'Jack is a great tribute to his family,' says Terry Tobin, 'because he's the one who had to do all the hard work, but he wouldn't have been able to do it without his grandparents. I've given him some advice along the way, mainly about his education, career choices and various projects he's been involved with, but Jack has made his own way in the world. That's what's so impressive about him. He's equipped himself well'.

Jack lives at Randwick in a unit owned by Chrissy's brothers, Jim and Greg Lee. 'We're still supporting him and always will, but he works part-time and pays his own way', Pat says. It is a quality Jack learned from his grandparents.

'The one thing that everyone who has had anything to with Pop all agree on, is that he has an unbelievable work ethic. It's amazing what he has achieved … a real rags to riches story … except it's taken more than fifty years to get where he is today and a lot of it is the result of hard work.

'When I don't feel like doing an extra shift at work, I always think to myself: what would Pop do? I don't want to let him down.'

Pat and Chrissy have introduced Jack to all their friends – they are impressed with the young man. 'I've been very close to Gai Waterhouse over the years and she knows of Jack's special circumstances', Pat says. 'He shares a birthday with Gai (2 September) and she's taken a great interest in Jack's progress. She takes him to lunch every year.'

Chrissy Webster grew up surrounded by music when she was a child and was determined that Jack have the same experience. 'I said to Jack, if you can learn to play the piano, everywhere you go you'll have friends', says Chrissy. 'The first three songs he learned were 'Advance Australia Fair', 'Waltzing Matilda' and 'Over the Rainbow'. Later came the Ella Fitzgerald and Patsy Cline songs.'

As a high-profile horse trainer at Sydney's racing headquarters, Pat also had his input. 'Pop would get up early and head off to the stables', Jack says. 'He has always had this great connection with his horses … I've seen him do some amazing things with these massive beasts. He has great control over them and absolute authority in what he does on the training track.'

Jack doesn't mind a bet and has cleaned up on Happy Clapper, but the training bug hasn't bitten him yet. 'He's been on track for every major race win, and we even got him up on stage after the Doncaster victory in 2018', says Pat.

There were 40,000 people on course the day Happy Clapper won the Doncaster in April 2018. As triumphant trainer Pat Webster made his way to the official podium, surrounded by well-wishers and besieged by backslappers, one voice could be heard across the fanfare of noise.

'Pop! Pop!'

'Jack was on course with a bunch of mates, but he didn't have access to the Members Enclosure', Chrissy says. 'Pat told them to jump the fence, but the ATC's Julia Ritchie saw Pat with his grandson, and ushered them through.' Jack ended up on stage with Pat during the presentation of trophies, and the veteran trainer was overcome with emotion in his speech.

'The love that poured out of Pat about Jack and what it meant for him to be there was unbelievable', Chrissy says.

'Star Casino were the sponsors of the race and they invited us back there to a function that night', Pat remembers. 'It wasn't really our thing, but we didn't want to be rude so we went and had a couple of beers to celebrate. It was a struggle to get there through the Saturday night traffic in the city but when we arrived, there was Jack with six mates drinking champagne in a roped off area. Typical St Joey's boys … where there's a free feed and a drink, they'll find it.'

'When Pop won the Doncaster, it was one of the best moments in my life', says Jack. 'I don't think I've ever seen him so happy. If anyone deserves to have a good horse, it's Pop. The best thing about Happy Clapper is what he has been able to do for Pop. The Clapper allowed him to achieve his dream.'

Jack is a bright, articulate young man to talk to, with a mature outlook on life that belies his age. 'Mine was a unique situation but it's all I've ever known. Nan and Pop formed me into the person I am today. I have a lot of their qualities too, which I am happy about, so they may as well be my mum and dad … it was the best situation I could have had and I wouldn't trade it for anything else.

'I use to wonder when I was younger why I didn't have a mother and father in my life, but as I got older, I realised how grateful I was for what Nan and Pop did for me. They gave me a great opportunity and sacrificed a big part of their life as well.'

There were times when Patrick Jnr's difficulties threatened to pull Pat and Chrissy's marriage apart, but raising Jack put it all back together again. 'We were at a bit of a low point', Chrissy admits. 'The pressure of Patrick's problems was taking its toll, but when Jack came along it regenerated our feelings for each other.'

Chrissy believes Jack came into Pat's life at the right time, just as Happy Clapper did. 'Only, having Jack in our lives is ten times better!' Pat adds.

And, at some deep level, Patrick Jnr sees Jack as his greatest achievement. 'Jack's a very special person and Patrick made him', Pat says. They have reminded Patrick of that fact a lot over the past five years as their son has slowly rebuilt his life.

But the Websters didn't take Jack to visit his father in gaol, so that the boy wouldn't have negative memories when Patrick got out and was looking to establish a relationship. Each year that he was in prison, Patrick would write his mother a letter and ask her to buy Jack a present from him.

'With Jack, there's Chrissy and me and no-one else', Pat says. Chrissy calls it the 'Jack and Pat Show'. 'He can certainly get around his Pop if he needs something', she says.

Jack says Pat reminds him of Clint Eastwood in the film *Gran Torino*. 'Pop's not a softy', he says. 'It's very much a case of tough love. But if you were going to have a mentor in your life, you couldn't pick any better than Pop. He proves that day in and day out with all the work he does with people affected by drugs and alcohol.

'I'm just lucky that he also happens to be my grandfather.'

'Pat is very generous to all his grandchildren', says Chrissy. 'He helps out when he's needed and is very generous.' But it is clear that Jack holds a special place in their hearts.

'Nan cares about everyone', Jack says. 'She's also very much a "no nonsense" parent, but she's on the other end of the spectrum to Pop. If I had a problem with schoolwork I would always go to Nan.'

Drive up to the Websters' farm at Kulnura on the NSW Central Coast and veer onto the track past the Ned Kelly letter box, and you come to a large gate at the entrance to the property.

'Pop gets to relive a little bit of his bush childhood up on that farm', Jack says. 'He's always loved the country and when he's up there, he's in his element. That's where he wants to be.'

And where Pat and Chrissy are happiest, Jack is never far from their thoughts.

On that gate is a handmade sign. It simply reads, 'Jack's Farm.'

CHAPTER 21

Racing Mates

Just before Christmas 2016, Pat and Chrissy got the news that Johnny Quinlan, a fellow apprentice jockey from the 1960s, a country trainer and their former neighbour in Mudgee, had taken his own life. Quinlan, age sixty-seven, had established a modest stable in northwestern NSW with wife Margaret, often working in the mines to supplement his moderate income. Margaret worked as his strapper, and also stacked shelves at Coles to make ends meet.

'I first met Johnny at Rosehill, where he was apprenticed to George Musson. Often, I stayed overnight at those stables after a race meeting, sleeping in the stable loft. George's wife was a fantastic cook.'

Pat talked Quinlan into transferring to Bernie Byrnes' stables, and they became great mates. 'Johnny was a good rider, but he broke his shoulder in a race fall and his career was over. He later moved to Mudgee and became a horse trainer.' Pat sent his mate some stable cast-offs to train, even recommending to him the services of his former apprentices, Sheree Gold and Joey Galea.

'Johnny loved a drink and a laugh. Walk into any pub in Mudgee and you knew he was there because of his distinctive laugh.'

Pat had a non-winner in his stables called A Million Roses. 'I sent the horse to "JQ's" and he won a couple of races with her. He then brought "Roses" down to the city and won a race at Canterbury with her.'

Pat and Johnny spoke almost weekly on the phone. 'When I had my success with Happy Clapper, he would ring me and joke about what a good a trainer he was. "Imagine what I could do with that horse", he'd say to me. "I got a win out of A Million Roses when you couldn't.'"

But Johnny Quinlan was a proud man, and never let on that he was struggling with depression – 'The Black Dog'. Pat certainly had no inkling. It still baffles him. 'I don't think anyone has any real insight into suicide – if we did, we could just flick a switch or take a pill and prevent it, and we can't. But we're more aware of it now.'

Suicide is the leading cause of death in Australian men aged 15-44. Men are three times more likely than women to take their own lives. Six Australian men take their lives each day and the number of suicides actually increased by 9 per cent between 2016 and 2017. Pat and Chrissy have had too much experience with that very human tragedy; their former apprentice jockey Johnny Hay, strapper Michael McCarthy, stable foreman Terry Mercer and now, close mate Johnny Quinlan, each took their own lives. That's why they got involved with the Racing NSW initiative 'Racing Mates'.

Racing Mates is a peer support initiative established by Racing NSW in 2016. The program includes morning teas and workshops across NSW country racing centres. Racing ambassadors such as trainers Pat Webster and Kim Waugh, former jockeys Rod Quinn and Kathy O'Hara, and current jockeys Emma Guymer and Cassie Smidt, provide a crucial link between those in need and the required support.

Racing Mates' 'get togethers' are held at various racing venues throughout the state and all industry participants – trainers, jockeys, owners, strappers – are invited to come along. Pat is also keen to 'lend his ear to others', as he colourfully describes it.

'It's a great opportunity for the racing community to come together for a chat', Pat says.

Research has found that effective support offered by peers and colleagues can aid significantly in coping with stress and difficult situations. Having access to clinical psychologists, counsellors and assistance hotlines is essential in helping others, and these services are made available to bush communities, but people are often more likely to initially reach out to a trusted peer or colleague for support.

'Sometimes we get the feeling at Racing NSW that we're just a band-aid solution but we're all trying to make a difference', Pat says. 'Beyond Blue, Lifeline, Boy's Day Out, Black Dog, Blue Elephant, Men of League … there is nothing better than talking to someone who understands where you're coming from.'

Empowering mates to look out for mates is their goal. 'If I can help someone, I've achieved what I wanted to', he says.

Pat is a racing ambassador for the Western NSW region. 'I love the bush because the bush gave me a start. I'll go to the track with Racing Mates and I'll see the people there and I feel for them. I've been there and done that with Betty Lane and Tiger so I know what they're going through.'

Bush trainers, he says, are 'salt of the earth' people. Interestingly, the success of Happy Clapper got him more acknowledgment from Sydney trainers than the bush trainers. 'Perhaps they don't read the papers', he laughs.

'When I do my trips with Racing Mates around the provincials, whether I go to Quirindi, or Dubbo or home to Inverell, most of the trainers there haven't even had a city winner so I'm happy with what I've achieved.'

That's why the TAB Highway races and the $1.3 million Kosciusko provides a pathway for Country NSW trainers to run their horses at Randwick and perhaps win a million-dollar race. 'It's all the bush trainers talk about', Pat says, 'Having a runner good enough for the city'.

With concern for mental health issues paramount in the bush, it's important that the racing community comes together when there's a tragedy. In April 2017, popular North West jockey Darren Jones was killed at the Warialda Cup meeting. The forty-eight-year-old was one of three jockeys who came down after a terrible fall in the Warialda Sprint (1100m). Keith Bullock from Racing NSW phoned Pat on that weekend with the bad news, saying Peter V'landys was personally asking him to go up to Armidale and talk to the jockeys there.

Jones had two young children, and many of his fellow jockeys were feeling for him.

Pat has lost too many good friends to racing accidents during his time in the game. 'Stan Cassidy was the first; he was killed when a rein broke in trackwork. Kenny Russell had a bit of luck with me, and we pulled off a couple of plunges together. He was killed in the last race at Rosehill in 1993. And then there's David Green and Noel Barker, who I both knew well.'

When a jockey is killed it sends a ripple through the entire racing industry. 'The country community feels it really bad. Darren lived in Tamworth and rode a lot of trackwork for the local trainers there. He was very popular and had ridden over 800 winners.'

The following Tuesday, Pat walked into the jockey's room at Armidale and asked if he could have their attention. 'I've been asked to come here and have a chat and a cuppa with you', he told them. 'If any of you have anything you want to talk about, I'll be here all day.' The jockeys gravitated to Pat, because they knew he would listen to them. He was like the Pied Piper, as one jockey later remarked.

Pat is very intuitive. He can read a room full of people very well. When he walked into the jockeys' room, he could sense the tension. 'People were sad, but were pretending not to be sad. I had a chat to a couple of Darren's close mates and they really opened up.' Pat talked to them about saddles and weights, tapping into their common experience as jockeys, before getting to the crux of the issues.

Pat often refers to himself as an 'ex-jockey' just in case his audience is too young to know that he once rode, 'because I certainly don't look like a jockey now. I talked to them about my fall, how lucky I was', he says.

'I sat down next to jockey Greg Ryan and asked who he thought was doing it tough and he suggested a couple of the young female jockeys who had a portable caravan out the back of the jockey's room. Without betraying any confidences, they missed their friend. Jones could give a jockey a spray if they did something wrong, but he was so respected.'

A percentage of all prizemoney from Racing NSW goes back into racing community welfare. That's where Racing Mates steps in. A trainer may be down on his luck, a jockey might be ill or there may be a funeral to pay for.

Pat is proud of the work he does. 'How often do you get the chance to say to a grieving family, or the widow of an old trainer that we'd like to help you out? It's a cross between playing Santa Claus and being an angel. I love it.'

The racing industry has changed in the last twenty years, he says. Racing Mates allows him to reconnect with the bush at a time when the Sydney racing scene is becoming increasingly competitive.

'A lot of the camaraderie has gone out of racing, and that's a bad thing. Les Bridge and I are the last of the original trainers from the 1970s – Ron Quinton was still riding winners when I started training in 1978.'

Not that he was ever tempted to leave Randwick and relocate to Wyong or Gosford, closer to where he now lives. 'Dad used to say you would give your right arm to train at Randwick and he was right. Once you've trained at headquarters it's hard to go anywhere else.'

Pat has seen the best and worst of human nature in racing during those years. 'There's a lot of professional jealousy in racing … too much in fact. That's hard for me because I'm not a jealous person.'

Some trainers wouldn't think twice about trying to take a good horse away from a rival trainer, he says. 'If you let the chooks out, I'll round them out', a leading trainer once told him. And yet, when his old Randwick neighbour Mal Barnes fell on hard times in the 1990s, the racing community banded together and raised $100,000 for his medical needs. Chrissy Webster was a driving force, along with journos Steve Brassell and Glenn Robbins.

And Pat is still a hard marker. 'To get respect as a trainer is hard work and, even today, people have to work hard to earn mine. When people ask me for advice, I am happy to give it but I was brought up in a very hard school of trainers ... and jockeys too.'

Be careful what you ask for because Pat will tell it to you straight. 'The goal is to survive, not accumulate Group 1 winners. Anytime I could pull off a betting coup I would do it to get some money for the family to live on, not for the glory.'

Webster is filthy that rival trainers may have used illegal methods to win big races. 'I thought the bad old days were over until the cobalt controversy', he says wearily.

And then premier Victorian trainer Darren Weir copped a four-year ban for using 'jiggers' – illegal electrical devices – on horses in his stable. Weir was the trainer of Tosen Stardom, who beat Happy Clapper in the 2017 Group 1 Emirates Stakes.

'Don't get me started', Pat says.

Pat has retained close ties with his Melbourne mates John Saddler and Robert Smerdon over the years. In May 2018, Smerdon was banned for life for 'systematically doping' his horses over many years with sodium bicarbonate 'milkshakes'.

'Robert got into trouble because he did the wrong thing, but I'm an old painter and docker and a mate is a mate', Pat says. The pair still talk regularly on the phone.

Pat believes trainers today don't tap into their peers enough. 'Cody Morgan rang me recently because he has a Teofilo colt in training, and wanted to know what the progeny are like. I told him what I knew about them, but we must have talked for 45 minutes on the phone. It was great.'

Pat still remembers what George Hanlon and Bart Cummings, now both sadly gone, taught him about racing. "If you struggle to break the last 400m (2 furlongs) in 26 seconds, you shouldn't be racing. Your horse isn't fit", Bart once said. 'How many young trainers today think that way.'

And what George Hanlon maintained: 'Cleaning out the feed bin is still the best indication your horse is right,' Pat says.

Pat has never been a big punter, and he believes this has driven a lot of decisions he has made about his horses. 'You become too close to your horses if you punt, and you end up betting on them when you shouldn't', he says. 'They lose, and you train them a little harder than you should and they lose again.' Instead, Pat attracted stable punters who gambled on his judgment with their money.

'I used my own money to pay my mortgage!'

It takes a special horse to make a man in his sixties get out of bed at 1.30 in the morning and head down the M1 to supervise trackwork at Randwick, but Happy Clapper was the horse he had been waiting all his life for. 'I was on the downward spiral before I got him but I've been able to be competitive without "the ball tampering" so to speak.'

It was frustrating waiting so long for a good horse, Pat admits, 'but then I remember that lots of trainers go through their whole careers without getting one. With Happy Clapper, I'm just blessed'.

But success does not necessarily breed success. 'After the Villiers and before the Epsom we didn't get one new horse', he says. 'I don't have a syndication behind me and I train at Randwick, which is more expensive than country areas. Gerry Harvey has always provided the "pick me up" if I needed one. I couldn't have done it without him.'

'I don't know why Pat doesn't get more horses because everyone who meets him loves the bloke', Gerry Harvey says. 'Perhaps it's because he doesn't market himself. He's a good bloke, and a good trainer, but a poor front man in that he doesn't promote himself or talk up his achievements. That's why Gai Waterhouse is so successful. Even Chris Waller, a quiet, shy bloke who shows his emotions, has the "X factor". But people can relate to Pat. I can't explain it …'

Brothers-in-law Jim and Greg Lee were able to market their careers at Hayai Lodge, named after their good stayer of the 1980s. 'It was bit late to for me in my sixties to market myself on Happy Clapper's achievements.' And at age sixty-eight, Pat admits he doesn't have the initiative to do it … to reinvent himself as a big 'factory' stable.

The hard truth is, Happy Clapper may just be the last horse Pat Webster trains.

Even with the emergence of a star in his stable, Pat knew that the training partnership with son Wayne wasn't going to last forever. 'It's a tough life', Pat says. 'The big stables in Sydney deserve all the success they have', he once told journalist Chris Roots. 'You're not just training horses; you're running a company. But the small trainer is only getting smaller.'

Wayne formed an integral relationship with the stable's new star, Happy Clapper. Pat liked to work Happy Clapper at 4 am before the other horses arrived. Son Wayne then did the bulk of the hard work during the day. 'If it wasn't for Wayne, Happy Clapper wouldn't be at the races', he maintains.

But not even the gelding's group success could put off the inevitable. 'I said, "Son, when Clapper retires that just might be the end for me. I can't train forever so you need to be looking around for something". I always tell my kids the truth – perhaps painfully so sometimes – and that's also why I don't have a lot of owners. I tell them when their horse is no good; whether it can win a race or not. Sometimes they take the horse to another trainer and three years later they ring me and say you were right about that horse.'

Wayne has made a lot of friends in the racing game, including John McGrath of John McGrath Real Estate and The Agency guru Matt Lahood. When McGrath suggested he start a cleaning company to service their real estate holdings, Wayne quickly came on board with good friend Anna Davis, the wife of Sydney Swans champion Nick Davis.

'John McGrath has been a great mentor for Wayne', Pat says. 'Matt Lahood is godfather to Wayne's son, Patrick.'

In racing, and in business, mateship is essential to success.

CHAPTER 22

The Clapper and Me

In August 2018, Pat Webster was invited to the NSW Racing's Night of Champions held at the Royal Ballroom at Randwick. Winx was once again set to dominate the awards, but having captured the Epsom-Doncaster double in the previous racing season, Pat's star Happy Clapper was sure to receive the Best Miler award. Not one to get dressed up for a night out, Pat was happy to delegate attendance to son Wayne to accept the award on the night.

What Pat didn't know was, he was also slated to receive the Media Personality of the Year Award. Always available for an interview and ready with a quote, the award was also recognition for Pat's work with young apprentices and his support of racing industry participants through the Racing Mates initiative.

It was left to the *Daily Telegraph*'s Ray Thomas to ring the veteran trainer to get him there on the night without giving away the real reason. 'Wayne was going to take Patrick along for the big night out, and then Ray rang, and said I should really come along too. I told him I didn't want to get dressed up and travel from the farm, but Ray added, "Pat, Peter V'landys would really like you to be there". And that was that.'

Pat is very appreciative of the role Peter V'landys has played in getting him talk to industry participants in need. 'Peter really cares about people, and as long as he's in charge, I'm happy to help out where I can.'

So, with Chrissy, Wayne and Patrick Jnr in attendance, the Websters walked the red carpet and Pat was awarded the industry voted prize.

'Happy Clapper's success has helped me enormously', Pat said on the night. 'I've been able to do a lot of good with my work with drugs and alcohol counselling because the Clapper put me on the map and gave me a platform to talk to people in need.'

On camera or in print, Pat is in his element. He is unflappable. 'Coming good in the same era as Winx meant that there was not that much extra ink used on Happy Clapper', Pat says. 'Perhaps the horse has been underrated. He's the only horse in history to win the "Big Three" miles at Randwick … the Villiers-Epsom-Doncaster. Throw in the Canterbury Stakes first up in race record time, and he's not a bad horse.'

Pat Webster, master of understatement.

'It always makes me wonder just how good the Clapper is because he's won first up at Group 1 level, and still raced competitively against Winx second up. The he came out the next fortnight and won the Doncaster. The horse is tough!'

Happy Clapper suited his trainer, but perhaps Pat had more influence on the horse's racing style than people have given him credit for. 'I think I'm a better trainer of horses up to a mile than out and out stayers because I'm a little too kind to them,' he admits, 'and my record shows that. Its common sense as long as you know your horse. You know what distances they like, how many trials they need'.

In the 'post-Winx era', Pat was looking forward to proving himself again as a horseman who could get Happy Clapper to be competitive as a nine-year-old, but he was going to take it just one race to the next. 'He hasn't been over-raced so the secret is to not work him too hard and to feed him well.'

He even toyed with the idea of starting the gelding in the Everest (1200m), the richest race in the world, which is run at his home track in October. 'He won the Canterbury Stakes over 1300m first up in 2017, which was a Group 1. He loves Randwick. He's competitive.'

But the Everest is invitation only, and as Pat admits, 'The horse can't get a jersey in the race. Not at his age'.

Happy Clapper began his 14th racing preparation the same as all the others … two trials at racing headquarters before heading to the races. Pat identified the Winx Stakes (1400m) at Randwick, the race formally known as the Warwick Stakes but renamed in honour of the great mare, who had won the race in the past three consecutive years. The race was also upgraded from Group 2 to Group 1 status when Winx won in in 2018.

Perhaps Pat Webster and owner Michael Thomas have an ironic sense of history, targeting the race named after their nemesis Winx. More likely, it was the fact that the Winx Stakes ticked all the boxes for the start of the horse's spring campaign … a Group 1 at the Clapper's home track. An ideal first assignment.

In June, Hugh Bowman's racing manager rang Pat and said that Winx's former jockey wanted to ride Happy Clapper in the Winx Stakes. Blake Shinn had taken up a contract with the Hong Kong Jockey Club and couldn't come back to Sydney so soon after settling there because it wouldn't be fair to his employers.

Perhaps Bowman, an old friend of Pat's and son Wayne, shared that sense of irony. More likely, he knew the horse would be competitive and he wanted to win the race for Pat.

Either way, Pat was confident the Clapper would return successfully. 'The Clapper is a very clean-winded horse anyway, and doesn't need too much work, but it's all based on what I learned from George Hanlon. Other trainers might think I'm probably a little too light on my horses – typically, a horse will have two trials then race itself into condition anyway. I'd rather do that than gallop them into the ground to get them fit.'

Happy Clapper was ridden by Hugh Bowman in two trials leading up to the Winx Stakes. In both trials, the Clapper finished out of the placings over unsuitable sprint distance. Was the horse back to his best, the media asked? In his second of these trials, the Clapper was only 1.7 lengths from the winner and was doing his best work on the line. Bowman hopped off the Clapper and reassured his worried trainer that the gelding was ready.

'I worry about all of my horses, but I drive people mad about Clapper', says Pat. 'The good ones have character, because we tend to look for it more, and Happy Clapper certainly has plenty of character. When Ainsley Fox pulls up at the stable on her motor scooter in the morning, he knows it's her … any other car pulls up, he doesn't even worry about it. But when the vet arrives, Clapper knows he's going to give him a needle and he walks over and hides in the corner.'

All good horses are sooks, Pat says, and the Clapper is no different.

'Oldtimers could look at a horse and just tell what was wrong with them', says Pat. 'Now we use blood counts. I get a lot of blood counts from Clapper, and he's not a good horse to get blood from. The horse drops his lip after going for a treatment and sulks in a corner.'

'Pat is an excellent trainer because the horse always comes first', says stable foreman John Burke. 'He's done it all with sheer hard work and determination. He's a real character, Pat. Put it this way: I'd go into war with the bloke.'

Happy Clapper follows a strict training routine, including being first on the training track every morning at 4 am. 'We don't swim him anymore because the experts say don't swim bleeders', says Burke. 'He works every day except Sunday unless he needs it. The Clapper is different to the other horses in the stable in that he is a good doer – he loves his food and is a good eater.'

Happy Clapper took his place in his 21st Group 1 race – exactly half of his 42 starts – on 24 August 2019. The first Group 1 race in Sydney in the new racing season, Happy Clapper's main rivals were the Godolphin-trained Avilius ($2.60) and the Oaks winner Verry Elegant ($5.50), trained by Chris Waller. The Clapper drew perfectly in ten-horse field in barrier 5, but drifted late in the betting to start $5.50.

In the lead up to the race, Pat was alerted to the fact that he had failed to tell stewards he was putting the blinkers back on Happy Clapper. 'I took them off in the Queen Elizabeth Stakes at the end of the horse's last campaign because I didn't want the Clapper to over-race after bleeding internally. I rang Chief Steward Mark Van Gestel to explain the oversight, saying that the Clapper racing without blinkers is like Superman without his cape.'

Van Gestel allowed the late gear change, slapping Pat with the automatic $200 fine. 'I then asked for extra time to pay it', Pat smiled.

Happy Clapper was relaxed in his stalls before the race, more relaxed than his anxious trainer and owner. Pat decided to remove the red earmuffs the horse normally wears in the parade ring in an effort to 'spark him up'.

'He was too relaxed!'

The pre-race plan was for Bowman to sit outside the obvious leader, the handicapper Samadoubt, or perhaps take the perfect sit, one out and one back. When the field jumped, Samadoubt took the lead, but with La Romain and Best of Days kicking up, Happy Clapper balanced up outside the fifth placed Invincible Gem. The leader was able to post some cheap sectionals before going for home on the corner, with Happy Clapper coming into the race three wide.

For a moment passing the 300m, Happy Clapper looked flat-footed as the gelding ground away into second place. 'At that stage I thought he would run fifth of sixth with the others swooping down the outside', Pat admits, but the Clapper dug deep under Bowman's urging and set out after Samadoubt. For a fleeting moment, it appeared the nine-year-old gelding might get there, but there was a half-length margin to Samadoubt on the line, with Happy Clapper posting yet another Group 1 second in front of Invincible Gem in third place.

Racing like the true miler he is, Happy Clapper was a touch dour behind the $31 outsider Samadoubt, who posted a race record time of 1:21.05 – faster even than any of Winx's three wins in the same race. After dismounting from the horse, Hugh Bowman said that the Clapper would have appreciated the sting out of the ground, but that the gelding had tried his heart out. The most important thing for Pat, going forward, was that the horse was sound and there was no recurrence of the bleeding attack Happy Clapper suffered the previous year.

'He's run a great race and showed us, even as a nine-year-old, that he's back', Pat told the *Daily Telegraph*'s Ray Thomas. 'We will probably go straight to the George Main Stakes (1600m) in a month. I'll give him a barrier trial before that.'

As much as a win in the Winx Stakes would have been the sentimental victory all Happy Clapper's fans wanted, and a perfect ending for this book, Pat Webster has been in the game long enough that there is no place for sentiment in sport … especially horse racing. Happy Clapper will race on, searching for another Group 1 win in a career that has already given so many people so much.

'That's racing', Pat says.

Whatever the future holds, there'll also be no more trips to Melbourne, and certainly no more tilts at the WS Cox Plate. 'There's a couple of sayings about Melbourne', Pat says with a twinkle in his eye. 'The Hume Highway heads out to Sydney and Tasmanians won't swim the Strait.'

Always the optimist, Pat still views his Melbourne campaigns as a success, however. 'The horse is Group 1 placed in Melbourne, but the icing on the cake for me as a trainer was Clapper taking his place in two WS Cox Plates. And while he was never comfortable in either race, he picked up $100,000 in prizemoney both times. But no, he won't go back there.'

Happy Clapper came along at a good time in Pat's life. Another one of Pat's many mottos is don't take success for granted because it's a lifetime coming. 'A good horse puts a spring in your step. I was ready to retire when Clapper came along, after keeping just 5-6 horses in work for so long. The Clapper puts a smile on my face because he proves there is still room for a trainer with a small stable at Randwick.'

That's the only sad part of the journey Pat has been on with Happy Clapper, in that one day it will end.

> **I still feel I have a lot to offer racing, but in my heart, I think that it's more with the work I do counselling and mentoring apprentices and being an ambassador for Racing Mates. That's why when Clapper is finished, I'll probably finish too.**

Pat Webster is a remarkable man. Success has not changed him, nor has it diminished his playful sense of humour and bush origins. He has worked hard for decades to build a comfortable life for himself, wife Chrissy and his children and grandchildren. He has also shown a remarkable talent as a horseman, working long hours behind the scenes at his Randwick stables, ensuring the horses in his care, and the people he employs, are at their very best – whether it be for a maiden at the provincials or a Group 1 race in the city.

When he retires, a whole lifetime of knowledge will be lost to the racing industry. That's why keeping Pat on as a mentor, counsellor and ambassador is so important.

'It'll be the end of an era when Pat gives up training', close mate John Singleton contemplates. 'I just hope we get a good horse before then. But no-one is under any illusions. As if running horses in circles is going to change the world? But the work Pat does behind the scenes is changing lives.'

'I've always kept my feet on the ground,' Pat says, 'and the older you get, the firmer the ground you search out. I'm going to miss the ride, but I'm not going to miss the pressure, the worry or the publicity, if you know what I mean.'

'I'm looking forward to putting my feet up. Just not anytime yet.'

20-Year Statistics: August 1999 - August 2019

Runners:	**1,921**
Winners:	211 (11.0%)
Second:	198
Third:	176
Placings	585 (30.5%)
Prizemoney:	$12,549,00
Group Wins:	15: 3 (Gr1), 4 (Gr2), 8 (Gr3)

Group 3 Winners

1999 – Frederick Clissold Stakes (Ab Initio)

1999 – TJ Smith Stakes (Ab Initio)

1999 – The Shorts (Ab Initio)

2000 – TJ Smith Stakes (Shy Hero)

2010 – Hawkesbury Gold Cup (Thankgodyou'rehere)

2010 – Gosford Gold Cup (Keepin' The Dream)

2011 – Bill Ritchie Handicap (Thankgodyou'rehere)

2017 – Newcastle Newmarket (Happy Clapper)

Group 2 Winners

1989 – Challenge Stakes (At Sea)

1999 – Challenge Stakes (Ab Initio)

2015 – Villiers Stakes (Happy Clapper)

2017 – Tramway Hcp (Happy Clapper)

Group 1 Winners

2016 – Epsom Hcp (Happy Clapper)

2018 – Canterbury Stakes (Happy Clapper)

2018 – Doncaster Mile (Happy Clapper)

HAPPY CLAPPER (bay gelding, b. 25.10.10)
Teofilo / Busking (by Encosta De Lago)

Age	Starts	First	Second	Third	(Unpl)
2YO:	1	0	0	1	(0)
3YO:	4	0	2	1	(1)
4YO:	4	3	0	0	(1)
5YO:	7	3	1	1	(2)
6YO:	9	1	2	0	(6)
7YO:	10	4	4	1	(1)
8YO:	6	0	2	0	(4)
9YO:	1	0	1	0	(0) *

Age	Starts	First	Second	Third	(Unpl)
GRP3:	4	1	1	1	(1)
GRP2:	5	2	1	0	(2)
GRP1:	21	3	7	2	(9)

* to 31 August 2019

CAREER RESULTS:

42 Starts: 11 wins, 12 seconds, 4 thirds

Prizemoney: $6,903,600

2-YEAR-OLD SEASON (2012-2013)

Kembla Grange, 20 July 2013

1200m 2YO MAIDEN HCP ($22,000)

1st - Kirov (Y Ichikawa 55.5kg)

2nd - Casino Dancer (W Costin 52.5kg) 0.2L

3rd - Happy Clapper (H Martin 54.5kg) 0.4L

Winning Time: 1:12.72, Barrier 4, SP: $5.00

3-YEAR-OLD SEASON (2013-2014)

Rosehill Gardens, 17 August 2013

1400m 3YO BM75 ($85,000)

1st - Aussies Love Sport (T Berry 56kg)

3rd - Happy Clapper (J McDonald 54kg) 2.3L

3rd - Kirov (H Bowman 58kg) 4.1L

Winning Time: 1:22.77, Barrier 6, SP: $4.20

Rosehill Gardens, 31 August 2013

1400m 3Y BM75 $4,150 ($85,000)

1st - Stamina (J Parr 55kg)

2nd - Bull Point (G Schofield 59kg) 0.1L

3rd - Savvy Nature (J Cassidy 54kg) 0.6L

* 4th Happy Clapper (T Clark 54kg) 1.2L

Winning Time: 1:23.75, Barrier 9, SP: $5.00

Newcastle, 18 September 2013

1600m GRP3 SPRING STAKES ($151,600)

1st - Savvy Nature (J McDonald 56.5kg)

2nd - Wordplay (P Robl 54.5kg) 1.5L

3rd - Happy Clapper (B Shinn 56.5kg) 1.6L

Winning Time: 1:36.37, Barrier 3, SP: $6.00

Randwick Kensington, 12 February 2014

1400m 3YO MAIDEN HCP ($40,000)

1st - Man of Melody (J Cassidy 57kg)

2nd - Happy Clapper (B Shinn 57kg) 0.2L

3rd - Fastcar (B Avdulla 57kg) 0.3L

Winning Time: 1:23.38, Barrier 9, SP: $1.95F

4-YEAR-OLD SEASON (2015-2016)

Canterbury Park, 26 January 2015

1250m 4YO+ NMW HCP ($50,000)

1st - Happy Clapper (B Shinn 56.5kg)

2nd - Isorich (T Marshall 55kg, Cd 52kg) 0.3L

3rd - Lolavie (T Huet 55kg) 0.5L

Winning Time: 1:14.39, Barrier 3, SP: $2.45F

Royal Randwick, 18 February 2015

1400m BM75 ($40,000)

1st - Happy Clapper (B Shinn 57kg)

2nd - Lassitude (S Clipperton 57.5kg) 0.2L

3rd - Bradman (T Clark 54.5kg) 1L

Winning Time: 1:22.22, Barrier 9, SP: $5.50

Warwick Farm, 4 March 2015

1600m BM80 ($40,000)

1st - Happy Clapper (B Shinn 56.5kg)

2nd - Lassitude (J McDonald 56kg) 0.5L

3rd - Excited Prince (T Clark 54.5kg) 1L

Winning Time: 1:35.73, Barrier 2, SP: $4.40

.... SPELL ....

Royal Randwick, 11 July 2015

1300m BM85 ($85,000)

1st - Idance (T Berry 55.5kg)

2nd - Lunar Rise (J Collett 57kg) 0.5L

3rd - Kristy Lee (T Angland 59kg) 3.3L

* 5th Happy Clapper (B Shinn 56.5kg) 4L

Winning Time: 1:20.49, Barrier 1, SP: $4.80

5-YEAR-OLD SEASON (2015-2016)

Royal Randwick, 24 October 2015

1200m BM85 ($85,000)

1st - Happy Clapper (B Avdulla 58.5kg)

2nd - Ryker (W Costin 57.5kg) 0.5L

3rd - Ziggy Willie (T Huet 54kg) 2.3L

Winning Time: 1:10.96, Barrier 5, SP: $3.00F

.... SPELL ....

Rosehill Gardens, 28 November 2015

1500m BM85 ($85,000)

1st – Happy Clapper (B Avdulla 60.5kg)

2nd – Final Decision (T Clark 55.5kg) 0.5L

3rd – Role Model (J Collett 57kg) 2L

Winning Time: 1:29.29, Barrier 2, SP: $4.20F

Royal Randwick, 12 December 2015

1600m GRP2 VILLIERS STAKES ($250,000)

1st – Happy Clapper (B Avdulla 53kg)

2nd – Tinto (T Clark 56kg) 1L

3rd – It's Somewhat (J McDonald 59kg) 1.2L

Winning Time: 1:33.98, Barrier 6, SP: $4.80F

Royal Randwick, 5 March 2016

1300m GRP1 CANTERBURY STKS ($500,000)

1st – Holler (J McDonald 56kg)

2nd – First Seal (B Shinn 57kg) 1.3L

3rd – Kermadec (H Bowman 59kg) 1.6L

* 4th Happy Clapper (B Avdulla 59kg) 2.4L

Winning Time: 1:15.4, Barrier 2, SP: $21

Rosehill Gardens, 19 March 2016

1500m GRP1 GEORGE RYDER ($1,000,000)

1st – Winx (H Bowman 57kg)   ·

2nd – Kermadec (Z Purton 59kg) 1.5L

3rd – Press Statement (J McDonald 56kg) 3.3L

* 5th Happy Clapper (B Avdulla 59kg) 5.2L

Winning Time: 1:28.7, Barrier 2, SP: $51

Royal Randwick, 2 April 2016

1600m GRP1 DONCASTER MILE ($3,000,000)

1st – Winx (H Bowman 56.5kg)

2nd – Happy Clapper (B Avdulla 50.5kg) 2L

3rd – Azkadellia (G Boss 50kg) 2.2L

Winning Time: 1:35.27, Barrier 8, SP: $13

Royal Randwick, 9 April 2016

2000m GRP1 QUEEN ELIZABETH II STAKES ($4,000,000)

1st – Lucia Valentina (D Oliver 57kg)

2nd – The United States (K McEvoy 59kg) 2.3L

3rd – Happy Clapper (B Avdulla 59kg) 2.8L

Winning Time: 2:04.82, Barrier 1, SP: $8.00

6-YEAR-OLD SEASON (2016-2017)

Royal Randwick, 3 September 2016

1400m GRP2 TRAMWAY HCP ($175,000)

1st – Hauraki (J McDonald 57kg)

2nd – Le Romain (K McEvoy 58kg) 0.8L

3rd – Dibayani (B Shinn 55kg) 0.9L

* 5th Happy Clapper (B Avdulla 57kg) 2.6L

Winning Time: 1:25.93, Barrier 2, SP: $8.50

Royal Randwick, 17 September 2016

1400m GRP3 BILL RITCHIE HCP ($125,000)

1st – Sons of John (B Shinn 55kg)

2nd – Torgersen (C Reith 54kg) 0.2L

3rd – Federal (C Williams 54.5kg) 0.4L

* 6th Happy Clapper (B Avdulla 59kg) 1.1L

Winning Time: 1:22.73, Barrier 5, SP: $5.50

Royal Randwick, 1 October 2016

1600m GRP1 EPSOM HCP ($1,000,000)

1st – Hauraki (J McDonald 56kg)

2nd – Dibayani (D Lane 54kg) 0.1L

3rd – Mackintosh (T Berry 52kg) 0.3L

* 4th Happy Clapper (B Avdulla 55kg) 0.6L

Winning Time: 1:33.87, Barrier 1, SP: $9.00

Moonee Valley, 22 October 2016

2040m GRP1 WS COX PLATE ($3,000,000)

1st – Winx (H Bowman 57kg)

2nd – Hartnell (J McDonald 59kg) 8L

3rd – Yankee Rose (D Yendall 47.5kg) 8.75L

* 6th Happy Clapper (B Avdulla 59kg) 11L

Winning Time: 2:06.35, Barrier 4, SP: $51

Flemington, 5 November 2016

2000m GRP1 MACKINNON STKS ($2,000,000)

1st – Awesome Rock (S Baster 59kg)

2nd – Hauraki (J McDonald 59kg) 0.75L

3rd – Seaburge (D Yendall 51kg) 0.75L

* 9th Happy Clapper (B Avdulla 59kg) 5L

Winning Time: 2:02.49, Barrier 12, SP: $16

Canberra, 5 March 2017

1400m NATIONAL SPRINT ($130,000) $25,000

1st – Gold Symphony (K McEvoy 54kg)

2nd – Happy Clapper (B Shinn 60.5kg) 1.8L

3rd – Handfast (B Avdulla 54kg) 1.9L

Winning Time: 1:22.66, Barrier 13, SP: $4.20

Newcastle, 17 March 2017

1400m GRP3 NEWMARKET HCP ($150,000)

1st - Happy Clapper (B Shinn 59kg)

2nd - Got Unders (J I Jnr 54kg) 3.46L

3rd - Kellyville Flyer (T Clark 54kg) 4.24

Winning Time: 1:23.79, Barrier 7, SP: $3.60F

Royal Randwick, 1 April 2017

1600m GRP1 DONCASTER MILE ($3,000,000)

1st - It's Somewhat (Z Purton 55kg)

2nd - Happy Clapper (B Shinn 55.5kg) 0.5L

3rd - Sense of Occasion (C Brown 52.5kg) 4L

Winning Time: 1:39.17, Barrier 2, SP: $7.00

Royal Randwick, 8 April 2017

2000m GRP1 QUEEN ELIZABETH ($4,000,000)

1st - Winx (H Bowman 57kg)

2nd - Hartnell (J Doyle 59kg) 5.3L

3rd - Sense of Occasion (C Brown 59kg) 5.7L

* 5th Happy Clapper (B Shinn 59kg) 7.7L

Winning Time: 2:07.22, Barrier 5, SP: $20

7-YEAR-OLD SEASON (2017-2018)

Royal Randwick, 2 September 2017

1400m GRP2 TRAMWAY HCP ($200,000)

1st – Happy Clapper (J Adams 57kg)

2nd – Tom Melbourne (M Walker 55kg) 0.8L

3rd – Invincible Gem (C Brown 55kg) 2.1L

Winning Time: 1:21.97, Barrier 2, SP: $5.50

Royal Randwick, 16 September 2017

1600m GRP1 GEORGE MAIN STKS ($500,000)

1st – Winx (H Bowman 57kg)

2nd – Happy Clapper (B Shinn 59kg) 1.3L

3rd – Foxplay (B Avdulla 56.5kg) 5.8L

Winning Time: 1:33.65, Barrier 7, SP: $15

Royal Randwick, 30 September 2017

1600m GRP1 EPSOM HCP ($1,000,000)

1st – Happy Clapper (B Shinn 57kg)

2nd – Tom Melbourne (G Boss 52kg) 0.5L

3rd – Snitzson (C Parish 50.5kg) 3L

Winning Time: 1:33.17, Barrier 2, SP: $2.40F

Royal Randwick, 14 October 2017

2000m GRP3 CRAVEN PLATE ($500,000)

1st - Classic Uniform (T Clark 59kg)

2nd - Happy Clapper (B Shinn 59kg) 0.2L

3rd - McCreery (H Bowman 59kg) 1.5L

Winning Time: 2:04.34, Barrier 1, SP: $1.50F

Moonee Valley, 28 October 2017

2040m GRP1 WS COX PLATE ($3,000,000)

1st - Winx (H Bowman 57kg)

2nd - Humidor (B Shinn 59kg) 0.4L

3rd - Folkswood (K McEvoy 59kg) 4.65L

* 6th Happy Clapper (D Oliver 59kg) 6.55L

Winning Time: 2:02.94, Barrier 8, SP: $31

Flemington, 11 November 2017

2000m GRP1 MACKINNON STKS ($2,000,000)

1st – Tosen Stardom (D Lane 59kg)

2nd – Happy Clapper (B Shinn 59kg) 1.5L

3rd – It's Somewhat (B Avdulla 59kg) 1.7L

Winning Time: 2:01.22, Barrier 5, SP: $8.00

.... SPELL ....

Royal Randwick, 10 March 2018

1300m GRP1 CANTERBURY STAKES ($500,000)

1st – Happy Clapper (B Shinn 59kg)

2nd – Global Glamour (T Clark 57kg) 1.3L

3rd – Invincible Gem (C Brown 57kg) 2.8L

Winning Time: 1:14.25, Barrier 1, SP: $4.60F

Rosehill Gardens, 24 March 2018

1500m GRP1 GEORGE RYDER ($1,000,000)

1st – Winx (H Bowman 57kg)

2nd – Happy Clapper (B Shinn 59kg) 0.8L

3rd – Kementari (B Avdulla 56kg) 1.6L

Winning Time: 1:31.48, Barrier 4, SP: $21

Royal Randwick, 7 April 2018

1600m GRP1 DONCASTER MILE ($3,000,000)

1st – Happy Clapper (B Shinn 57kg)

2nd – Comin' Through (T Clark 51.5kg) 2L

3rd – Arbeitsam (M Dee 50kg, Cd 51kg) 2.2L

Winning Time: 1:33.17, Barrier 1, SP: $5.00

Royal Randwick, 14 April 2018

2000m GRP1 QUEEN ELIZABETH II STAKES ($4,000,000)

1st – Winx (H Bowman 57kg)

2nd – Gailo Chop (M Zahra 59kg) 3.8L

3rd – Happy Clapper (K McEvoy 59kg) 4.1L

Winning Time: 2:01.65, Barrier 9, SP: $11

8-YEAR-OLD SEASON (2018-2019)

Flemington, 15 September 2018

1600m GRP1 MAKYBE DIVA STAKES ($752,000)

1st - Grunt (NZ) (D Oliver 58.5kg)

2nd – Kings Will Dream (IRE) (J Allen 59kg) 2L

3rd – Jon Snow (NZ) (S Baster 59kg) 2.5L

* 5th Happy Clapper (M Zahra 59kg)

Winning Time: 1:34.91, Barrier 12, SP: $8.00

Caulfield, 1 September 2018

1400m GRP1 MEMSIE STAKES ($1,000,000)

1st - Humidor (NZ) (DM Lane 59kg)

2nd – Kementari (G Schofield, 8) 58.5kg) 0.1L

3rd – Kings Will Dream (IRE) (J Allen 59kg) 0.2L

* 7th Happy Clapper (M Zahra 59kg)

Winning Time 1:23.29, Barrier 7, SP $6.00

.... SPELL ....

Royal Randwick, 16 February 2019

1400m GRP2 APOLLO STAKES ($256,000)

1st – Winx (H Bowman 57kg)

2nd – Happy Clapper (S Clipperton 59kg) 2.3L

3rd – Egg Tart (B Avdulla 57kg) 4.3L

Winning Time: 1:20.88, Barrier 1; SP: $11

Royal Randwick, 2 March 2019

1600m GRP1 CHIPPING NORTON ($605,000)

1st – Winx (H Bowman 57kg)

2nd – Happy Clipper (B Shinn 59kg) 1.8L

3rd – Unforgotten (K McEvoy 57kg) 5.6L

Winning Time: 1:33.27, Barrier 3, SP: $9.50

Flemington, 16 April 2019

1600m ALL-STAR MILE ($5,000,000)

1st – Mystic Journey (A Darmanin 54kg)

2nd – Hartnell (GB) (W Buick 59kg) 1.25L

3rd – Alizee (H Bowman 57kg) 1.35L

* 8th Happy Clapper (B Shinn 59kg) 3.8L

Winning Time: 1:34.77, Barrier 8; SP: $4.00

Royal Randwick, 13 April 2019

2000m GRP 1 QUEEN ELIZABETH II STAKES ($4,000,000)

1st – Winx (H Bowman 57kg)

2nd – Kluger (T Berry 59kg) 1.5L

3rd – Hartnell (K McEvoy 59kg) 4L

* 4th Happy Clapper (B Shinn 59kg) 6L

Winning Time: 2:02.54, Barrier 6; SP: $31

.... SPELL ....

9-YEAR-OLD SEASON (2019-2020)

Royal Randwick, 24 August 2019

1400m GRP1 WINX STAKES ($500,000)

1st – Samadoubt (T Clarke 59kg)

2nd – Happy Clapper (H Bowman 59kg) 0.5L

3rd – Invincible Gem (R King 57kg) 0.8L

Winning Time: 1:21.05, Barrier 5; SP: $5.50

(All statistics courtesy Racing NSW)

ACKNOWLEDGEMENTS

Thank you to the Webster family, especially Pat and Chrissy Webster for their friendship and hospitality in the course of writing of this book, and to their children, Patrick, Diane and Wayne, and grandson Jack.

Thank you also to Gerry Harvey, John Singleton, Michael Thomas, Terry Tobin, John Burke and Jack Dixon for their interviews.

Thank you also to New Holland Publishers, especially Fiona Schultz, Elise James, Arlene Gippert and Yolanda La Gorcé. Lastly, thank you to my family for the patience and continued support.

ABOUT ALAN J. WHITICKER

Alan Whiticker was born in Penrith, in 1958. Pursuing the dual careers of teacher and freelance writer, he emerged as an award-winning author of sport, history, biography and true crime. In 1997, he completed a Master's Degree in Education and lectured at the University of Western Sydney in 2008. He then worked as an author, commissioning editor and international publisher.

Over the past two decades, Alan has ghosted books with John Laws (*Well, You Wanted to Know*, 2017), Dawn Fraser (*What I Learned Along the Way*, 2013), Shannon Noll (*So Far*, 2012) and Jimmy Barnes (*Say it Loud*, 2002), as well as various rugby league players (Royce Simmons, Cliff Lyons, Terry Lamb, Mat Rogers and Luke Lewis). He has also written extensively on true crime, including books on the Wanda Beach Murders (2004), the disappearance of the Beaumont Children (2006), serial killer Derek Percy (2008) and the impact of the murder of Anita Cobby (2015).

Alan is also a published author of history and pop culture, including *Speeches That Shaped the World* (2005), the *British Pop Invasion* (2015), *The Classics: The Greatest Hollywood Films of the 20th Century* (2016) and *Classic Albums: The Vinyl That Made a Generation* (2018).

Now a full-time writer, Alan lives in Penrith with his wife Karen.

HAPPY CLAPPER

THE
ALL-STAR
MILE